YOU WILL OFTEN FIND THAT when you have a vision, you don't see the road to the vision; you just see the vision. Maybe you are struggling with seeing clearly the path that lies before you. Don't even worry about it. Sometimes, it's okay if you don't have the full journey plotted and mapped out.

You figure it out as you go along. That's how it was for me. *Sweet Expectations* is the story of my journey, of how I took my great-great-grandmother's unusual legacy, the legacy of a woman who was born a slave, and made it into my personal recipe for success and self-determination. It's the story, too, of the legacy I've created for my own three daughters and my granddaughter, and all the sacrifices I've made along the way—as well as all the triumphs that have kept my hope alive.

I'd like to share with you the landscape of my journey. It is often a winding road, complete with sharp twists and turns, to which I am certain you will be able to relate. The school of hard knocks was a blessing for me—maybe it will be for you, too.

I really believed early on that you write your own destiny— that you actually have the pen to write your life. Sometimes you run out of ink. Sometimes you have to get it refilled. Sometimes you have to get a new pen altogether, but you're always, always, always the writer. I really believe that.

SWEET EXPECTATIONS

Michele Hoskins' Recipe for Success

MICHELE HOSKINS
WITH JEAN A. WILLIAMS

Adams Media
Avon, Massachusetts

Published by
Adams Media, an F+W Publications Company
57 Littlefield Street, Avon, MA 02322. U.S.A.
www.adamsmedia.com

ISBN: 1-59337-205-1

Printed in the United States of America.

J I H G F E D C B A

Library of Congress Cataloging-in-Publication Data
Hoskins, Michele.
Sweet expectations / Michele Hoskins with Jean A. Williams.
p.   cm.
ISBN 1-59337-205-1
1. Michele Foods. 2. Hoskins, Michele. 3. African American businesspeople—
Illinois—Biography. 4. Businesswomen—Illinois—Biography. 5. Syrup industry—
Illinois. I. Williams, Jean A. II. Title.
HD9330.S874M534 2004
338.7'6641—dc22
2004011395

This publication is designed to provide accurate and authoritative information with regard to
the subject matter covered. It is sold with the understanding that the publisher is not engaged
in rendering legal, accounting, or other professional advice. If legal advice or other expert
assistance is required, the services of a competent professional person should be sought.
—From a *Declaration of Principles* jointly adopted by a Committee of the American Bar
Association and a Committee of Publishers and Associations

Many of the designations used by manufacturers and sellers to distinguish their products
are claimed as trademarks. Where those designations appear in this book and Adams
Media was aware of a trademark claim, the designations have been printed in initial
capital letters.

This book is available at quantity discounts for bulk purchases.
For information, call 1-800-872-5627.

There is no royal flower-strewn path to success. And if there is, I have not found it for if I have accomplished anything in life it is because I have been willing to work hard.

*—Madam C. J. Walker, nineteenth-
and early-twentieth-century
African-American entrepreneur,
philanthropist, social activist*

To my mother, my father, my two brothers,
my three wonderful daughters, my granddaughter,
and my two devoted dogs Gizzy and Lady.

—M.H.

For Keith Simmons, my late brother.
Your love and Keishanda, your sweet daughter, sustain us.

—J.W.

Contents

Foreword

I MET MICHELE WHEN SHE WAS a panelist during a Women's Foodservice Forum luncheon in Chicago. I was truly touched by her remarkable story and, like so many others, felt compelled to introduce myself to her. A year or so later, we attended a businesswomen's retreat where the focus was on "being true and real"—first to oneself and then to others. Michele's whole life is a portrait of being true to yourself, listening to your inner voice, your own drummer, and being focused on your dream and making it a reality.

As I've grown to know and respect Michele since meeting her more than six years ago, I've discovered that she is very much like her great-great-grandmother, whose recipe for syrup is the genesis for Michele Foods. She has a great sense of family pride, of passing along important life lessons, of being supportive, and of being present and involved in the lives of her loved ones.

In some cases, she's learned from the school of hard knocks (and hard "nots"), but through it all she has remained a positive, graceful, and reflective woman. While her company is her life's blood, sweat, and tears, her heartbeat is her family, friends, and treasured business associates. They are the most critical elements in her "Recipe for Success."

I've had the pleasure of spending a lot of time with Michele over the past few years. We've shared so many things, yet reading *Sweet Expectations* showed me that I didn't really have an appreciation of the seemingly insurmountable challenges she's faced. This book provides insight into her personal drive, motivation, and her strong spirituality. Michele has a genuine appreciation for those who have supported her and she's learned important life lessons from those who were a source of angst in her life.

I've learned that my friend Michele is an example of an American business success story, a victorious woman's success story, and an example of success of the human spirit.

Sweet Expectations shares the ups and downs of building a business from the bare minimum. It shares lessons of sales, finance, brand building, production, and retailing. It's a guide for effective networking, building a strong support base, and negotiating effectively.

It's a wonderful journey that shares the importance of family, spirituality, being compassionate, and giving back to others. *Sweet Expectations* is delightfully delicious.

—Pat Harris,
Chief Diversity Officer, McDonald's Corporation

Acknowledgments

A PERSON'S LIFE STORY is so much more than words on a page, pages in a book, or a book on store shelves. I truly needed a publisher that was sensitive to this truth. I had been approached to tell my story several times before Adams Media came along. The fact that you are reading this acknowledgment is a testament to the fact that they won my trust and I believed that they were up to the task. The entire Adams Media team has come to be special to me; everyone has been very gracious, very professional, and very excited about this book. But I'd especially like to show gratitude to Kate Epstein. Without her, *Sweet Expectations* would never have happened.

Aside from the Adams Media team, I'd like to thank writer Jean Williams. Jean stepped into my life and won my confidence. It is not easy to open up to a stranger and tell her twenty years of your life, including the highest highlights and the lowest lowlights. It took great patience and understanding on both our parts to make it work in a short period of time. Thanks, too, to Hermene Hartman and David Smallwood of

Chicago's *N'Digo Magapaper* for the wonderful cover story they did on me and for directing me to Jean.

Thanks as well to all the great people I've met in the food industry—on all the boards I've served on, the organizations I've spoken before, and the conferences I've attended. Each and every experience has contributed to my growth and to my success and my knowledge of this business. I would especially like to acknowledge my experiences with such people as John H. Johnson, Oprah Winfrey, and Jesse Jackson.

My wonderful family deserves the highest thanks, especially my three girls, who are always there for me. I am ever grateful to Rosalyn, who is my oldest and my friend and someone who I know will do anything for me. Christale, who is my friend and partner in business, is someone I can count on at any time, day or night, to listen to me and to advise me. Keisha, my youngest daughter and good friend, keeps me laughing and smiling through some of our darkest moments with her positive attitude.

I'd also like to thank my loving parents, who have believed in me and encouraged me through some of my hardest times and have held my hand through some of my most harrowing experiences.

God bless you all!

Introduction

SO OFTEN IN OUR LIVES, we look but do not really see. We listen, but do not truly hear. And we know, but do not actually realize. The simplest truths often are the least self-evident and it can take a lifetime to mine the most precious jewels of wisdom wrought by the constant, seemingly sudden revelations of realities that were always there to begin with.

Often, the hardest truths to come by are the ones that are closest to home. It seems that the mirror gets foggier the harder we peer into it.

In my travels and in growing Michele Foods, my family business that manufactures pancake syrup that retails in more than 10,000 stores nationwide, I have seen my own image in dozens of newspapers and magazines, including *Essence, Black Enterprise, People, Fortune,* and even the *National Enquirer.* I've also proudly made it to that mecca for people who aspire to all manner of achievement: *The Oprah Winfrey Show.* I have been featured three times on the show for my proverbial rags-to-riches life story. Yet no matter how many times more I see myself depicted and written about in the mass media, it always pales in comparison to the first time I ever *really* saw myself. Or the first time I *truly* heard what God was leading me to do. Or the first time I *actually* realized that I had all that I needed to change my circumstances.

Ironically, the real Michele Hoskins came to the light in some of my darkest days. It is often said that adversity introduces us to ourselves. I had been familiar with this saying all my life, but never truly heard it until my own life became the flesh and blood embodiment of it.

Now I know intimately: Not only does adversity introduce us to ourselves, it introduces us to others as well. There were people in my life who thought, as I had, that they knew me down to the core. But I later showed them that they hadn't even scratched the surface, for I discovered that at my center was a deep layer of mettle—the stuff that steels us for the shake, rattle, and roll of life. When we tap into it is when we find what we're really made of, and it gives us a clue as to how far we can really go.

Before I hit my center, I didn't think I could go anywhere. In the late 1970s and early 1980s, my husband and I were splitting up. We realized that our marriage was just not working. His main concern during the divorce was my ability to take care of our children financially. His concerns were well founded—I couldn't pay the mortgage loan and feed the children with my income. I was devastated, and for a while, at wit's end.

But I would soon learn that this wasn't the whole truth about me. There was so much more to be seen, heard . . . realized.

I discovered the path to renewal in something that had been right before my eyes all my life. A generations-old family tradition would be my saving grace: my great-great-grandmother's legacy—a secret family recipe for the best syrup anyone I knew had ever tasted. The tradition in my family, set by my great-great-grandmother herself, had been to pass the recipe on to the third daughter in each generation. Though I was not the third daughter in my immediate family but the *only* daughter, I persuaded my mother to let me hold the recipe for my own third daughter, Keisha.

As I was coming close to hitting rock bottom, it occurred to me that it was time to get more mileage out of my great-great-grandmother's legacy. I decided to market the syrup. I had no idea whatsoever about how to do it, but it was all I had. So I went with it, blind with ignorance at the same time that I was enlightened with hope and prayers.

Ultimately, I established Michele Foods, which is now a multimillion-dollar business. Today, I can see clearly the labyrinthine path that I took to get here. But back then, I could see little of it on the horizon, which was probably a good thing in the long run. I was rocked to my core on more than one occasion, including the days my kids and I spent on welfare as I pressed on to build the business, overcoming a life-threatening illness, and waging a knock-down-drag-out fight with white-owned food industry conglomerates that bought products like mine on a daily basis to the tune of millions of dollars annually, but initially refused to do business with me.

There were many other episodes that struck me to the core. With each one, I realized again that I could make it;

I could survive. And with each challenge, I have gotten to see myself anew, to hear God's intentions once more, and to realize that there's still so much more yet to my story.

I'd love to see you on the road to success. Perhaps my story will provide you with somewhat of a compass for your own journey. Or, who knows, maybe you might even hitch a ride with me. It just could be that I'm going your way.

Fight for My Life

THE DOCTOR IS SPEAKING NONSENSE TO ME. Although his words actually make plenty of sense when you get right down to it, I am baffled nevertheless. It's 1993, and for one whole year I have been having constant, throbbing headaches of migraine intensity. They came on gradually. At first, I'd have them, and then I didn't. Now, however, I wake up with them, and I go to sleep with them. Eventually, my vision faded as the headaches worsened. I've been to all sorts of doctors and healing types, but to no avail. Finally, I have landed here, in the plush Magnificent Mile offices of a headache specialist with offices in Chicago's luxurious Water Tower office and shopping complex.

This specialist has come highly recommended by my primary physician, who is also my gynecologist. He is lettered, accomplished, and has a solid medical reputation. But he might as well be a shock jock today. I am just crushed as I listen to his diagnosis. "You have a massive growth on your brain," he says. "It's on your pituitary gland, and it's pushing on your optic nerve."

My brain? My optic nerve? I think about the foggy cloud through which I have grown to see the world as my eyesight has gone to the dogs. That must be some monkey of a tumor, I think, lying inside my head like a brick and stealing my very vision.

It makes sense, of course, but I can't help but seek deeper meaning than medical logic—because you have this tumor, you have these headaches and you are losing your eyesight. You see, to me this diagnosis somehow feels like a verdict as well, something I began to wrought somewhere long ago. I've always tried to be a positive person, but I believe that something that I allowed—the fear of failure that I've known I could not afford, ever since I decided to start my own business in 1984—has actually manifested itself in my head.

And it's something I don't care to deal with just now. So I don't much care right now about the specialist's professional pedigree. I just want him to have a good follow-up to the zinger he just handed me.

But what he says next only confounds my fears. "We need to operate immediately."

Well, how do you react when someone tells you something like that? This just isn't the time for a massive growth to be in my head of all places. I am already in the middle of massive change, and change is a constant in my life by now. I have finally found an investor to help expand my nine-year-old syrup manufacturing business, which has had more than its share of upheaval. Helping it through this next phase of change is the only massive thing I want to make room for in my life right now.

Soaking in the doctor's pronouncement, I react as I suspect anyone might. I become visibly upset. I cry and cry. The doctor directs me to a private room nearby where I can be alone for a few moments to begin to sort out my feelings. I go in and cry some more. Then I call my parents, and I ask them to come and get me.

After much of the smoke clears, I begin to have a clearer perspective. My intuition returns. Somehow I begin to sense that I will be fine. Now, I still have fear. I just balance it with a healthy sense of positive thinking. It's not easy. I must fight to push aside those nagging fears that are by-products of horrible tales I've heard. You know the ones: So-and-So went into the emergency room with a simple headache or a stomachache and never came out again. John Doe went under the knife and never woke up.

Thankfully, years prior to this ordeal I had opened myself up to new ways of thinking. As a younger woman, I was introduced by a good friend to Buddhist thought and philosophy. It was at the most perfect time, too. I had been in search mode for a while, and the self-actualization aspects of the religion appealed to my natural instincts. I had already begun to develop an appreciation for the belief that, basically, you reap what you sow. I believed then, as I do now, that we all go toe-to-toe with the karma in our lives.

I also believe that through sheer will and positive thought I can fight back, that by putting mind firmly over matter I can beat this thing. I just have to mind my thoughts, to attract a positive outcome.

So when the specter raises that I could have as little as nine months to live, my gut instinct tells me that, despite all this doctor knows medically, he does not have a clue about me. He does not know, for instance, that I have made something of practically nothing. That I have taken a quaint family tradition—a recipe for pancake syrup—and turned it into my daughters' legacy. That I was told too often to count that I could not do it. That I did it anyhow. He does not know that I spent much of my life being someone other than the woman sitting across from him. That I had been reduced to whatever roles I could play in the well-being of others. That I have evolved so that I now play some of those same roles as well as others of my own choosing. That I have stamped out the parts that didn't fit the new definition of me.

He doesn't know these things, and I am not inclined to hold it against him. What I am inclined to do is glove-up for a good fight.

By the time my parents arrive to pick me up from the doctor's office, I've already gotten back my resolve. It's late on a Friday. In the coming days, a lot will happen and fast. There will be an operation bright and early Tuesday morning. They will go into my head and remove the tumor. By Wednesday, I'll be in recovery. This isn't even going to compare to what I've already come through. I'm certain of it.

Chapter One

A New Sense of Purpose

Men can starve from a lack of self-
realization as much as they can from
a lack of bread.

—*Richard Wright, novelist*

I REMEMBER THE RAIN. It was a light drizzle, but it was persistent. I was staring out the window of my condominium
on the South Side of Chicago. It was a quiet day. I had a fire
going, and the kids were doing their homework. My husband
wasn't home. And I was sitting at this window—a huge bay
window in the living room that I really liked—thinking about
how much I really didn't like my life.

I don't know if I sat there for one hour or four. And I
don't remember what was going on around me. I can't tell
you if the stock market was up or down, or what was the
number one song in America. I just know that on that day in
1981, I experienced a significant moment of change. It wasn't
going to bring the world to its knees, this change. But it
would soon have its way with life as I knew it.

This didn't all happen spur of the moment. It had been a long time coming. Inch by inch, I had arrived at this point, at this moment of change: It was time for me to get out of here. There was a trip I needed to take, and I had to pack my bags—literally and emotionally.

A New Way of Seeing My World

Looking around my home, I saw the irony of it all. I had loved this place. My husband and I and our three girls lived on South Shore Drive in a very large three-bedroom condominium overlooking Lake Michigan. It had a wood-burning fireplace and beautiful hardwood floors. It was comfortable, cozy, and well decorated. I have always had a flair for interior design. I like nice things, and I had done a pretty impressive design job.

But that's just it. This apartment and its contents were about as impressive as it got when it came to my accomplishments. I kept redecorating, thinking that would make me happy. Then I'd want a new car. I felt limited and unfulfilled, and no matter how much or how often I changed my surroundings, I couldn't fill the void inside of me.

For years, I had felt trapped in my own life. I had gotten married very young, before I knew who I was. When you're that young, you are not concentrating on who you are; you're concentrating on things that are in your environment. For me that became marriage and children. For some people, this is utopia. It was utopia for my mother, and I always thought that it would be for me, too. I mentally scanned the apartment.

"This has to go," I knew. "All of this materialistic stuff has to be shed." It was all attached to this predestined world that I no longer wanted any part of. I didn't want the couch. I didn't want the pictures. I didn't want the silverware. And I didn't want to be married.

The Layers of My Life

I wanted to pick up the phone and talk to a girlfriend about this. But there was no one I thought would truly understand. I had friends and associates, but as I contemplated changing everything about my life, I didn't think there was anyone I could trust. If I had a girlfriend, and we were friends because we had domestic things in common, how would she react if I wanted to get rid of those domestic things? If I had a friend that I'd known in high school and stayed in touch with through college, who had known the me I'd become by following everyone else's expectations, how would she react if I wanted to become someone completely different? The way I was thinking just wasn't in anyone's thought pattern at the time. I felt like a fish out of water.

I had not grown up in a time when women were encouraged to be independent. Women were not encouraged to be the breadwinners. Women were not encouraged to be single parents. The American dream was to finish high school, go to college, get married, and have babies—women take care of babies, while husbands go out and work.

Beyond my own social circle, there was change on the

horizon, but it was slow to arrive. There was still fallout from the Vietnam War. People had to change, including women. Men had come back from the Vietnam War with no legs and women had to figure, "I've got to work. My man is now disabled." It was a turning point in history. But the people around me weren't quite ready for me to be part of that.

Getting divorced and remaking my life reflected how I felt. My family and friends all thought I had lost my mind. They thought I was being rash. But from where I stood, there was no stepping stone out of this world and into a new one. I had to take it all off. I had to strip down to what really mattered—to be naked again in a sense.

Each of us is born naked—literally without a shred of clothing. We are also naked in the figurative sense. We have very little knowledge of anything. We are shaped and molded by everything and everyone in our lives. I was no different. I had always lived my life as a product of my environment. It seems the only way I could see myself at all was in the reflection in someone else's eyes—someone else's expectations. I had been someone's daughter. I had been someone's sister. I had been someone's wife. I had been someone's mother. But I had never really been me.

As a grownup, you have to find your own way in this world. And this, to me, is all I was doing. I was declaring that I now wanted to take charge of my own destiny. Instead of changing the drapes or the carpet, I was going to redesign my own life, to create my own expectations for myself—and those would be sweeter than anything anyone else had ever devised for me.

To fill the void inside of me, I would have to get rid of all of the things I had tried to fill it with before. Even Gemini, our family dog, had to go. He had been given to me as a gift—an accessory to this domestic world of mine. So I eventually handed him off to a neighbor. (I later regretted getting rid of Gemini. Today, I have two dogs who are like family to me, and I would never voluntarily part with them.)

My young daughters—Rosalyn, Christale, and Keisha—were the only attachments I wanted from this world. Holding them close, I would go forward and create a new life for us all.

Maybe you're like I was that day when I watched the rain and sat by my favorite window. Maybe you have a vague sense that you're not happy in your life, even though everything might be perfect from a certain point of view, and your life might be someone's idea of utopia. You might not have to lose everything, like I did. But get ready to re-envision the core of your life, to find your own utopia.

When I got up from that window, I was ready. The process began that very day. I was ready to chip away at this prefabricated world of mine. I knew there had to be something more than this for me.

SUCCESS INGREDIENT ONE

Be open to change, and be ready to embrace it—change can wreak havoc on your life, but it can also bring you life's greatest gifts.

Chapter Two

Working Girl

You can never be happy living
someone else's dream.

—*Oprah Winfrey, talk show pioneer, actress,*
producer/creator, magazine founder and
editorial director, educator, philanthropist

I HAD NOT LIKED BEING A HOUSEWIFE. After my husband moved out, I needed to find a job. I took a part-time job teaching world religion at Aquinas Catholic High School. I taught school because the schedule allowed me to be with my daughters.

There was no job security in teaching, especially for me. I wasn't teaching math. I wasn't teaching English. I was teaching world religion, which made me more expendable. If they were cutting out courses, mine wasn't one that they would likely keep. So it wasn't a stable job. Plus, the Catholic schools at that time were disintegrating at a rapid rate.

So I was always saying to myself, "You know, this is not a stable lifestyle. Do I go back to school and put four more years into it . . . to be what?" I had to stop and figure out how

I would handle a setback. I was like, "How can I emerge out of everything that's going on with me and be successful?" I didn't immediately have answers.

I quit teaching and worked various other part-time jobs so that I could take care of my girls. First I worked for a company that made a hand cream of mink oil. I worked for them for a while as a salesperson in a department store, but I didn't feel connected with them and quit. Then I took a job working for the federal government with the U.S. Department of Education, where I helped to track down people in default on their student loans. Later, just as I was beginning to launch Michele Foods, I would work at Carson Pirie Scott department store, which would prove a turning point for me. But none of these jobs made me happy.

The Wrong Workplaces

It was true that I hadn't liked being a housewife, but I also didn't like working for someone else. What frustrated me with most of my jobs was that I had to stay until they told me I could leave. I did not like that. I did not like punching a clock. I wanted to go home, and I couldn't.

I did not like being in these environments. I felt like I didn't belong there. Some people are comfortable with these worlds. I was not one of them.

Later, when I started Michele Foods, my life would be far more stressful than it had been, and I would work much harder than I ever had before. But I didn't mind it in the same way that I had when I punched someone else's clock. Once I was working for myself, all the stress and hard work seemed worth it. It's easy for me to see how every little bit extra that I do for my own company benefits me, very directly. And for my own employees, I try to keep a sense of balance between working hard and having fun together—and to always reward hard work.

When I looked at my check from each of my early jobs, I never felt rewarded for my hard work. I would think, "I'm working for this amount? This is what you're making?" And I couldn't make any more without working overtime, which would mean more of my time. I just wasn't the individual to earn a living in this way.

It wasn't just the little bit of money I was making. But I knew that if you want to be rich and successful, you can't do it working for someone else. When you work for other people, you are contained within their guidelines. You're who they need or want you to be. You're filling in a gap. Things are pretty much predetermined for you. You're walking into a job description.

I wanted to create my own job description, and really live up to *that*. I was already breaking out of confinements in my personal life. I wasn't going to stop with career confinement. I had gone to college in the early 1970s because it was part of what my parents expected of me. I hadn't really been thinking I would be out working afterward, because of course I expected to be supported by a man, just like everyone always expected that for me.

One after another, the jobs I got were just more ways that other people would try to make me live up to their expectations. And making so little money, working so hard, feeling so stressed—it wasn't worth it if I was going to have to do what my boss wanted to do anyway.

So there I was, a young, educated African-American female who was uneducated to life. If my job no longer existed, what else could I do? Finding meaningful employment could be tough, especially for a black woman. You had to figure out what you wanted to be.

A Eureka Moment

While I was going through the divorce and working one part-time job after another, I made a discovery that would be extremely important in shaping my destiny. I read in an article that the '80s were the decade of the woman. The article said that the decade was going to turn out independent, successful women. Corporate America was going to open up. Women were going to be CEOs of companies. Women were going to be entrepreneurs. It was a time when, if you were a woman and you were going to be something, this was it. There were a lot of resources available to women. The article was right: By 1992, a third of U.S. firms would be woman-owned (according to the U.S. Census Bureau).

I thought about it. I was going through divorce proceedings. I had three small children. I did not like any of the part-time jobs I had held. I did not like working for someone else. I was at a point in my life where I was saying, "What do I want to do with the rest of my life?"

I decided to become an entrepreneur. I did not even understand what an entrepreneur was—I had to look it up in the dictionary—but I could get enough from the article to know: I wanted to become an entrepreneur. I wanted to be independent. I wanted to be able to raise my children without always struggling for money. I wanted to be able to control my own destiny. I wanted to join these powerful women who would dominate the '80s.

If you're like me, and you're unhappy living in the confines of what someone else thinks you should be, and punching someone else's clock makes you crazy, you have to be grateful that you live in a world with expanded opportunities. Because this is the least you need to remake your life.

So now all I had to do was come up with how I was going to use this entrepreneurial energy. Whatever I was going to do, I had the urge for it to be remarkable. I needed it to be extremely different from all that I had experienced thus far—and all that had been expected of me.

SUCCESS INGREDIENT TWO

Be ready to listen to *eureka* moments. The most unexpected sources can show you the way to transform your life and create your own destiny.

Chapter Three

The Discovery of My Mission

Your work is to discover your work
and then with all your heart to give
yourself to it.

—*Buddha Shakyamuni,*
founder of Buddhism

MORE THAN ANYTHING ELSE, I believed my daughters—my three baby girls, who weren't such babies anymore at the time—needed a mother who was doing remarkable things. I grounded my efforts in this belief. My girls were at very impressionable ages back then. I detested the idea of them coming of age believing that they always had to make their desires subservient to someone else's—even mine.

Thinking about my girls in this way, wanting to be the best role model I could be, it occurred to me the answer to what I could sell was right here in my family.

My Great-Great-Grandmother's Unusual Legacy

I come from a family of cooking women. I mean they *really* cooked. I was the only daughter and was around my mother a lot. So, of course, I learned to cook, too. From early on, I had one of those little Easy Bake Ovens. (In fact, I had all the girly, domestic toys.) I didn't particularly like cooking, but it was definitely something that I was destined to learn. I didn't have to cook for the family when I was growing up. My mother took care of that. But she made sure that I learned.

My mother had this recipe that had been handed down in our family from my great-great-grandmother. The recipe was for pancake syrup—we called it honey cream—and the tradition was that the third daughter in each generation would get to have it. It was to remain a secret to everyone else.

My great-great-grandmother was named America Washington, and she was born a slave in the 1860s. She worked for a family that did not like molasses on their pancakes. So she created a syrup for them. The syrup was made of churned butter, cream, and honey. America decided, for some reason, to pass down the secret recipe to only the third daughter of each generation. No one knows why she picked the third daughter—I imagine that maybe her third daughter was *her* favorite. Maybe she was a third daughter herself.

My mother was a third daughter, so she ended up with the recipe. When I was growing up, I thought that it was the only syrup around because that's all we ate. We didn't eat Mrs. Butterworth's or Log Cabin. Nor did we eat any prepackaged pancakes. My mother was the type of cook who made everything from scratch. The pancakes were from scratch. The biscuits were from scratch. And the syrup was from scratch.

In fact, back then, probably most of what crossed the table was from scratch—breakfast, lunch, and dinner. You have to understand, my mother is in her late eighties. She didn't have a lot of the convenience foods that we have now.

And our family traditions of having fresh, hot, honey cream syrup went right along with that. It was just something that was always there. When I was growing up, my grandmother was alive. We would go to my grandmother's house, and she would talk about her mother giving her the recipe. So it was a family tradition. And being a family tradition, it was often talked about.

Everyone talked about honey cream syrup. As I grew, I came to take great pride in this family recipe—not a lot of African-Americans have anything from their ancestors that far back. But like most of the family, I had only consumed the syrup over family breakfasts. I didn't know how to make it. My mother had gotten the recipe from her mother because she was the third daughter. Well, I was the only daughter in my immediate family. I was not supposed to be let in on the secret. But for a long time, I was curious about that recipe. I would always ask my mother to share it with me. She would say, "I'm still alive. I'm cooking with it. Don't worry about it."

I had eventually persuaded her to let me "hold" the recipe for my own third daughter, Keisha. So I was accustomed to making the syrup, too. I would make it and invite people over for breakfast. They would always say how good it was.

The Start of My Own Legacy

So after I had read this article that said women would rise in the 1980s, and decided I wanted to be an entrepreneur, it occurred to me that the syrup was good enough to market. The tradition had been to pass down the recipe to every third daughter. I thought, "I could hand my girls a business instead. That would a better legacy than a recipe."

This is where the process of Michele Foods, Inc., started. It started at one of the lowest points in my life. I was going through divorce. I was unhappy in my job. I had three small children to care for. I was young—just going into my thirties. I didn't know anything about what I was about to do. But I was going to be doing what I wanted with my life finally. I had done everything everybody else wanted me to do. As a child, I had gone to Catholic churches and schools. I had gone to college. I had gotten married and had children. I had worked jobs that were unsatisfying. And all the time, I had felt that I was in bondage. So it's ironic that the legacy started by a slave woman, my ancestor, would help to liberate me. But at this point, all I had was this recipe, the passion to do this, and growing faith in myself. I did not have the business experience to go with it. I didn't know anybody who had started a business. No one in my family had been an entrepreneur. My father had been a butcher, and my mother had been a postal worker. I didn't know anybody in this world that I wanted to enter.

I didn't know much, but I knew one thing. I was going to do this. No one was going to stop me. America Washington, a woman born a slave—my great-great-grandmother—was calling out to me. It's like she reached out from the past and said, "I've been waiting for somebody to realize that this is more than a recipe."

From Bondage to Liberation

I had my mission. I had set my sights on being an entrepreneur with the family recipe. I began to get glimpses of the vision. Early on, I started to visualize my dream. From my raw thoughts, I could see the bottle of syrup, and I imagined all of the stores. But outside of my head, no one else bought into it. And my personal life held many obstacles to my progression toward starting a business.

My husband was fighting me for custody of our girls. It was a move that was uncharacteristic for the times. Sure, fathers seek custody all of the time nowadays, but in the early '80s, it wasn't common. My husband was in school studying to become a lawyer. I think he must've been inspired by that 1979 film *Kramer vs. Kramer*, in which Meryl Streep and Dustin Hoffman fight in court for custody of their son. He made an issue of my employment status. I was a part-time teacher, and he questioned how I could manage caring for the children with that income. On top of that, I was retaining two lawyers, one to handle the divorce proceedings and one to handle the custody battle.

My husband underestimated me, because I was not giving up my children. Nor was I giving up my dream, which was inspired by them. Children can be your best motivation and your best inspiration. I did not want my daughters to have the same limitations that held me back. I wanted them to know from the outset things it took me years, a marriage with a man who wasn't right for me, career dissatisfaction, and emotional trauma to figure out. I knew I couldn't keep them from their own share of hard knocks in this world. But I would at least give them the benefits of my struggles.

With all of this going on—family and friends doubting the moves I was making, me being unhappy as a teacher, and my husband fighting me for the kids—I held on through faith. I locked in on my vision and wouldn't let go. I was in this for the long haul.

The secret syrup recipe was legendary in our family. Little did I know, growing up and even throughout my marriage, that it would become key to my personal emancipation and evolution into the Michele Hoskins I desperately needed to be.

I know mine is an unusual situation. Most people can hardly point to anything that was left to them by their ancestors, let alone a recipe for a marketable product. Most African-Americans, in fact, can't even claim to have gotten their own names from their ancestors. But you see, my great-great-grandmother left us a recipe. I began to see that it was up to me turn it into a different legacy: a formula for success.

You could be missing a gem gleaming right before your very eyes. Someone may have left you a powerful legacy that you can't even see. They may have left you with the by-product of a bad situation, for instance, like my great-great-grandmother having to keep a plantation owner's family happy—and that might be a potential gold mine.

SUCCESS INGREDIENT THREE

Sometimes the key to your success is right in front of you—sometimes it's something that you've known since you were a little child.

Chapter Four

The Success Formula

I got my start by giving
myself a start.

        —Madam C. J. Walker, nineteenth-
        and early-twentieth-century
        African-American entrepreneur,
        philanthropist, social activist

I WAS VERY NAIVE when I first started formulating Michele Foods and my products. I would have to pull it all off through faith.

Not knowing the best place to start, I just started the best way I could. My first instinct was to invite others in on my plans. I picked up the phone and called my brother. I called my best girlfriend. I called several other friends of mine. I wanted them to be a part of this vision that I had. I said, "We're going to start this company." They sort of humored me at first. We would have these meetings every Wednesday at my house. First we had six people. Then there were three people. Finally, there was just me.

Everyone thought that it was a very crazy idea that I could start my own company, and it was not something that they thought I should try—let alone that they should join in with me.

It seemed so logical to me. We could do this together. We could all reap the benefits. They just didn't take me seriously, though. It was not something that they wanted to do.

My Own Way

"What are you doing?" my family and friends were asking. "I mean, you're talking about divorce." My husband and I had separated.

"You're talking about quitting your job?" There also were a lot of people trying to persuade me not to do this. Divorce proceedings were underway. It would be awhile before I would leave the work force altogether, but I was already considering that step. I stood steadfast, and I told everyone, "This is what I want to do."

So I had to be okay on my own. I didn't bother hunting down all the reasons why people didn't take to my ideas or my vision. Entrepreneurship is for the risk-taker personality—someone willing to go it alone. And those people are usually pumped up on their vision, which can be very personal. Even today, my daughters say to me about Michele Foods, "This is your vision." And they're right. It is my vision; it's not theirs, and I can't make it theirs. They work at the company, but it is not based on their vision.

And so it was, I found out that this was not something that I was going to drag a lot of people into. It became clear; I had to do this on my own.

A Taste of Reality

Along with vision I had what I call the three Ps—patience, passion, and perseverance. When I decided to put the syrup on the market, I thought that I could make it up on the stove, put it in a bottle, and sell it. So that is what I did. Soon after, however, the knowledge came to me that this wasn't the way to do it at all. I had skipped a few steps—a bunch, I would learn.

I used to eat breakfast on a fairly regular basis at a small restaurant on the South Side of Chicago. It was a family- and community-oriented neighborhood spot, and I often took my daughters with me. I believed that this was a natural first stop for my syrup. I knew the owner. She was an African-American woman. So I prepared some syrup, and I put it in a jar. I called it Supreme Products, and I made up a little handmade label. I took the syrup in to her, and asked if she would buy it from me and serve it to her clientele. She sat down with me at her table, and said, "Okay, Michele, I'll serve it tomorrow morning with breakfast and see how people like it."

The next day she called me. There was a problem with the syrup. It had turned rancid. She told me that I could not sell it like that. So that was my first realization that this was not the correct way to market this product.

I was disappointed, but not discouraged. Most people would say, "Well, let me go and do something else." You can't do that if you're going to succeed. I went back to the proverbial drawing board. I said, "No, I'm not quitting. This is what I want to do, so let me figure out how to do it." I'm very spiritual. So, of course, the first thing I did was pray, and I asked God for some guidance. I kept asking, "Okay, how do you do this?" It came to me that I should pick up the phone and start dialing for answers. I went through the Yellow Pages, and I started calling all kinds of businesses, including chemical companies. I ran across a gentleman who told me that in order to get any food product into the retail market, the product must first be formulated. With that piece of advice, everything shifted.

I had to figure out what that meant exactly. I eventually learned that it meant the syrup needed to be made so it can withstand time—have a shelf life and stability.

Unexpected Help

I had talked about my ideas in detail with my mother. Like everyone else, she had found it hard to see my vision at first. But now that I had reconciled the idea that I was going it alone, she slowly warmed up to the idea. Once I had convinced her that I was completely serious, she started to let her guard down. Eventually she said, "Well, if you're going to do this, you might as well try to do it right."

She told me that she had read an article in the newspaper that might help me. A company called Resources was looking for food industry entrepreneurs, people who had unique recipes and wanted to put them on the retail market.

"Here it is," she said, handing me the article. It was from the *Chicago Tribune.*

I learned that Resources had helped a gentleman put a chili product on the market. It was called Dudley Davenport's Frozen Chili, and his grandmother had given him the recipe. Resources offered an umbrella of services and had actually helped him formulate and develop his product. The company had been so enthusiastic about their success with him that they were looking for other food industry entrepreneurs with a good recipe and similar energy that they could help start a company. They needed entrepreneurs to apply with recipes so they could determine which would be best to push.

They were located in downtown Chicago. I made some syrup, and I took it to them. This would be my first real contact with someone who could help me with this process. After my meeting with the group, they felt that out of the 250 applicants that had applied to them for help, I was the one who had the best recipe that could be formulated for retail sales. So they invited me in. They provided a chemist, a product developer, and a graphic designer for me to work with.

But there was a snag. They said, "You have to raise your own capital. We've got everything else, but we don't have any money." And I didn't have any either. But that did not stop me. I said, "Okay, great. We don't have any money. So what do we do now?"

The first thing I did was call my brother, and I said, "You know what? I need $25,000."

I knew he would need more information, so we went downtown to Resources together.

After that trip, my brother agreed to lend me $25,000. So now, my mother was coming around and my brother was lending me money. It was almost as if my family was now saying, "Well, if she's going to do it, we might as well not abandon her totally. Let's try to help her. We're not going to sell the family jewels, but we will help her a little bit so she can't come back and say, 'You all didn't help.'"

And so the process officially began. Dealing with Resources made it feel all the more real.

SUCCESS INGREDIENT FOUR

Find the right people to help you on your journey—and be patient with those who might be resistant at first. They can't always see your vision.

Chapter Five

A New Source of Inspiration

Success is liking yourself, liking what
you do, and liking how you do it.
—*Maya Angelou, writer*

THE WORKINGS OF RESOURCES gave me a glimpse into the
kind of workplace I wanted to be a part of. These were
entrepreneurs that I was dealing with, independent people.
They were like little busy bees in their own world, controlling
their own lives. Even though they were all providing services
under this umbrella called Resources, they were creative
people who set their own hours. I noticed that the graphic
designer, for instance, would be working at 7 or 8 P.M. But
when she didn't choose to come in—because she was traveling or doing something that she wanted or needed to do—
she didn't come in. Or maybe she was working on other
projects with other clients outside of what she did with
Resources. I hadn't seen this sort of setup before.

Around this time I would find a job that taught me even
more about the kind of environment in which I could thrive.

Working It Out

The reality at the end of the day was that, even as I pursued my dreams, I still needed to make money the old-fashioned way: I still had to work for someone else.

While my husband and I struggled with each other—and various lawyers—in divorce proceedings, I struggled with ways to earn a living part-time, care for my daughters full-time, and start a business with the syrup recipe.

A turning point came while I was working at Carson Pirie Scott department store. I met a group of interesting people there, including Roosevelt Cartwright, who would later become Oprah Winfrey's makeup artist. Roosevelt worked for John H. Johnson's Fashion Fair Cosmetics as a makeup artist. We became friends and I helped him get into an apartment in my condo building. Later, through Roosevelt, I met a man who was vice president of Fashion Fair, a line of cosmetics especially created to serve the needs of African-American women. He and his wife had just moved to Chicago from New York. Later, the VP of sales offered me a job working as a makeup artist and retail sales associate with Fashion Fair Cosmetics. I accepted the job and it became the one job that finally got me up in the morning with something I had never had before: passion.

Though I had never been in sales before, I would soon discover that I was a natural. Plus, I was assigned downtown at the Marshall Field's department store Fashion Fair counter. I liked the exciting environment of a department store. This would be a better job than all the others, but my primary goal was still to get into business for myself.

A Sip of Freedom

Working at the Fashion Fair makeup counter was my first taste of freedom as someone else's employee. And I actually liked what I was doing. I was glad to see that you can get up every day and work, but have a passion for something. And I had a passion for getting up every day, going to Fashion Fair. It was like an awakening for me because it was like I'd finally found this slight hole to get through to the other side. I'd finally found a way out of my situation, and it was something that I could get up and do every day.

I was in Marshall Field's, so there was some regulation there, but still, I was in a world where I controlled my time. If I wanted to go on break, I could go when I wanted to go. I knew there was limited time I could take, but that was welcome discipline to me. It made me reason, "Okay, here I am. I appreciate the break, but I understand how getting back to work as soon as possible benefits me." So I was enthusiastic about getting back to work. Sometimes I didn't even take a break! Sometimes I worked all day. I was even enthusiastic about working overtime because I controlled the paycheck. I had learned to really understand the relationship of sales to commission. I understood that if I made $4,000, only a small portion of that would be mine. But I could sit and reason, "This week, I'm going to try to make $1,000 in commission," or whatever the magic sum.

I liked that I didn't know what was going to happen each day. There were things I could expect, of course. I knew that I could go there one day and have $1,000 in sales, or I could go there one day and not sell even one thing. It was mainly up to me. That felt like controlling my destiny to me.

So working at the Fashion Fair makeup counter kind of set me up for this world that I was getting ready to get into—this world of running my own business. It made me understand, "On one end, if you go to work and don't open your mouth, you don't make a dime. But if you go to work and really put something behind it, you'll make enough money to pay the bills and to put enough money aside for your own business."

Aside from not having to be chained to a desk, I also liked that the job's hours worked well enough so that I could care for my daughters. I could come to work at 9 A.M. and at least I could be home by 4 or 5 P.M. And at that time, Rosalyn was old enough to take Keisha to school, and Christale, my middle girl, was old enough to take good care of herself.

Having the Fashion Fair job didn't get my husband off my back, though, nor did it solve my financial problems. So I had to buckle down. Later, when I moved back home with my mom, he and his lawyers began to back off a bit. Yet I found myself constantly hostage to a judge. But you had to be a really bad person for the courts to take your kids from you. Thankfully, they weren't too concerned about my income. They could see that I was a good mother.

Sales Success

Fashion Fair taught me one of the most important lessons I would take to my own business: great selling ability. I could expect that every day I was going to encounter lots of people. While at Fashion Fair, I also learned how to interact with people from different social classes, careers, and countries. The job taught me how to be very personal with all types of people. I learned how to talk to people. I learned how to listen, too. I learned how to understand a person's needs. Understanding these things at a makeup counter was preparing me to be someone who would be able to sell syrup. I was molding this person without help from anybody. No one said, "Well, this is how it goes, Michele." This was all new to me. I had to find my own way.

Pretty soon, I was on a roll. Women at that time were into lots of vibrant colors and eye shadow, but I was more into skin care. I've always been into good skin. I've always been kind of a health nut, always telling people that drinking water is important and it's needed for great skin. So instead of pushing the latest color, I started talking up the Fashion Fair skin care treatments, which included a cleanser and toner. If a woman with bad skin came to me and said, "I want my face made up," I would say, "Well, you know, if you go and use the treatment for two or three weeks and come back, it'll look so much better when I apply the makeup." So while most of the other makeup artists and sales associates were selling $8 lipsticks and $10 blush, I was getting women excited about having good skin, and they were buying skin care treatments for $45. Sometimes a woman would buy as much as $200 worth of Fashion Fair products.

I was doing lots of business for Fashion Fair. When I would go home and talk about this, the reaction was, "Wow!

That's fantastic, Michele!" I was called into the Fashion Fair offices. My supervisor wanted to know: "When you work, sales are $3,000 a week as opposed to someone else's $800. What are you doing different?"

"I teach customers about skin care first and makeup second," I said. I explained to them that my teaching background made it easy for me to provide clear instructions and to answer questions thoroughly.

They were enthused about my success, but this special attention was the beginning of my end with Fashion Fair.

SUCCESS INGREDIENT FIVE

The best way to reach people—whether you're selling something, or teaching something, or motivating someone to do their best work—is to listen and learn to see a situation from their point of view.

Chapter Six

Early Role Models

God puts people in your life to
teach you lessons.

—John H. Johnson, entrepreneur

JOHN H. JOHNSON, the owner of Fashion Fair Cosmetics,
was my first entrepreneur role model. Like I always say, in
life you're either a student or a teacher. At this particular
point, I became a student learning from Mr. Johnson—a legendary African-American multimillionaire who had renown
and a great human interest story.

Mr. Johnson, the owner of Johnson Publishing Company,
Inc. (publisher of *Ebony* and *Jet*), created Fashion Fair Cosmetics in 1973 to offer cosmetics for the needs of African-
American women. He had started Johnson Publishing—the
largest African-American-owned publishing company in the
world—in 1942, starting with a $500 loan on his mother's
furniture.

I had read his magazines and used his lipsticks, but to
actually see the man close up and personal was priceless. I was

enthusiastic about working for Mr. Johnson, and I was very enthusiastic about selling his products. I thought, "These are *his* products. He's thought them out, developed and manufactured them, and he's put them in my hands."

There I was, on the verge of launching my very own products. I couldn't have paid for a better education. I could look at this man and be inspired by him directly. It made me think, "If Mr. Johnson can do it, why can't I do it?"

Finding the Cultural Connection

Even in the early 1980s, African-American entrepreneurs were few and far between. I also admire Madam C. J. Walker, an African-American woman who was the first multimillion-aire woman in hair care, in the early 1900s. In her day, black men were hardly even working in jobs and she had started her own company. She had people working for her, fancy cars to drive, and was very respected. Her story pulled at me, beckoning me out of the confinement of who everybody thought I was. And I was starting to really develop into who I was going to be.

When I was working for Mr. Johnson I didn't even imagine that I would receive the first Madam Walker Spirit Award, one award of the many I've received that I feel particularly blessed by. I had long admired the accomplishments of Madam Walker, the free daughter of slaves who made her fortune in hair care products. The award was presented to me by A'Lelia Bundles, Madam Walker's great-great-granddaughter.

I couldn't ignore the fact that we're both great-great-grand-daughters of women who are such forces in our lives today.

But Mr. Johnson was the closest I had come to actually knowing an entrepreneur. So I was excited about this job and being so close to his accomplishments. Though he was not a close, personal friend, he became someone pivotal in my journey nevertheless.

An Education in Entrepreneurship

I also got to see what Mr. Johnson's success had manifested for him. In attending meetings, I had gotten to see the inside of his building, located in downtown Chicago—which many people only got to see from the outside. I had lunch in his cafeteria. All of these things helped me to consider all of the possibilities.

Plus, I got to see firsthand the kind of leader Mr. Johnson was. He was an imposing presence. To be frank, his people feared him to some degree. He was very hands-on and wanted to be personally accountable for all aspects of his business. Even though he was a successful person, there were some things about him I did not want to mold myself after. I did not want to be feared, and I wanted my employees to know they could be honest with me. I knew even then that you have to define for yourself how you want to lead. This all goes hand in hand with setting your sights on the mission and then trying to understand each step of the mission.

When I started working in sales at Fashion Fair, I had all kinds of questions teeming in my mind. I was curious about how the product was manufactured. Did Mr. Johnson own a cosmetics plant? What went into the product launch? What were his distribution strategies? Understanding all these issues and understanding how Mr. Johnson's company handled them would prove priceless down the line.

I had a good view to see what he was doing. I could learn a lot from him. I could watch how he moved the product. I could watch how he advertised it. I could watch how he promoted it. I could watch how he gave away things. I could watch all the different things that he did to make his product successful. I learned a bit about how inventory worked. Sales reps would come up to me and would say, "What are you out of?" And I had to know so that I would have ample supplies.

I didn't really know it at the time, but I was absorbing all of it. And all of it would be useful in my own business.

A Whole New World

I was trained to apply and sell makeup at Fashion Fair, and I was picking up a good deal about entrepreneurship. But there were other lessons for me at Fashion Fair. For one, I learned how to dress. Before this job, I had primarily been a housewife. I was at home mostly, and I wore jeans, a shirt, and gym shoes. I took my kids to school, and I came home and

I cooked for them. When I was a teacher, I wore working-class clothing. It was pretty much the same when I worked for the government and on the other odd jobs I had held part-time.

But there was a different dress code for Fashion Fair. This was a glamorous world to me. In it, I would regularly see and interact with businesswomen who came up to the counter. I saw beautiful clothes on the department store's racks all day. I would go up to the eighth floor and see furs. I could go up to the ninth floor and see furniture. And it started making me say, "This is what I want."

I started visualizing and seeing the type of clothes I wanted to wear and the type of furniture I wanted in my home. I was imagining a particular lifestyle in my head. I knew even then that this was how you did it. You conjure your vision and then you release it and let it happen.

The job also put me in the position to meet interesting people in downtown Chicago. A young Oprah Winfrey was one of the most memorable.

A Fateful Meeting

The first time I met Oprah, in 1984, she walked into the Marshall Field's department store on State Street. One day I said to her, "I'm going to put a product on the market." She said, "You go, girl! One day we're going to cross paths."

I said, "Okay, we are," and I believed it would happen because she said it. Even then, there was something about her.

I would see Oprah after that from time to time walking down the street. She used to walk out of Channel 9, where she was doing *A.M. Chicago,* the popular local talk show that preceded her hugely popular national talk show, *The Oprah Winfrey Show*.

Meeting her was exciting for me even back then, before she became phenomenally successful. Even her local success was astounding. She was a bona fide sensation in Chicago before the rest of the world was let in on our secret. I was glad to be in an environment where I could meet such an interesting person, and her example and her faith in me was an inspiration to me from the time I met her.

SUCCESS INGREDIENT SIX

Find the people who will inspire you to realize your own potential, and listen well.

Chapter Seven

The Necessary Violence of Change

I believe that the greater the
handicap, the greater the triumph.

—John H. Johnson, entrepreneur

SO NOW I WAS LEADING a double life at Fashion Fair and moon-lighting to get my syrup to market. All the while I was selling Mr. Johnson's products, Resources was progressing with getting the syrup ready for retail. But, of course, they needed more money than the $25,000 that I had borrowed from my brother.

Every time I would go into their offices downtown, it seems they needed more money. They would say, "Okay, Michele, we've formulated the syrup. We need $16,000 to go to the next step. You need fact sheets, and here's a man who could do them for you." Or they'd say, "Bring your daughter and your mom to take pictures for the marketing material. But it's going to cost you $2,300 to do the photos, and then you've got to get them printed up."

In all, I determined that I would need $150,000 to continue to the point where the syrup was a marketable product. That's when I made a drastic decision. I knew I had no one else to turn to, so I would have to turn back to me. I thought, I might as well sell what I own to raise capital. So that's what I did. I told the kids, "I'm selling the condo. I'm selling the car. I'm selling the furniture. I'm selling everything, and we're going to move back home with my mom. I'm going into business for myself."

So I started selling things. Every time Resources needed more money, I would find something else to sell. I sold my engagement ring. And the girls and I moved into my mother's attic.

Stripping Away My Protection

It seemed as if everything that was familiar and secure was dissipating, and here I was starting a business. I had sold my condo and traded in my nice car for an older, used one that looked and felt as if it had been in a few accidents. A lot of stuff was going on.

But I knew it was all part of the master plan. These are the kinds of risks and responsibilities that entrepreneurs typically must take on. An average person who has average responsibilities—a household, husband, and kids, or what have you, may reason him or herself out of dreams such as mine. He or she may think, "Now here I am, a person who went from having my mama and daddy taking care of me to now having my own responsibilities, which is to take care of my kids. They didn't abandon me, so I cannot abandon them. So I've got to go to work. I would love to do this other thing, but for now I'll just dream about it."

That defeatist attitude keeps a person right where she is. A person who steps out of that boundary will say, "Okay, here I am going through divorce with three kids. I can't pay the mortgage, so I'll just sell everything right now while it has some value to it, and I'll put it into this product." That's what I did. I sold my furniture, my car . . . my everything to raise the money.

When I decided to do this, the only attachments that were necessary were my girls. Everything else could be eliminated. Everything else was materialistic. When I walked into Resources' offices, I wasn't planning to sell my house, my worldly possessions, and move back home to my mom's attic. But when I walked out of there, and I had to make a decision; getting rid of my things became part of the equation. If I had been attached to a bunch of decision-makers going, "Oh, I would never do that!" then I would never have even tried.

To be successful, you have to step out of the norm because the norm is following a pattern and not realizing that you're stuck in something. You have to go it alone in a sense.

These are just things that I had to do. I had to come up with money. Any time I didn't come up with money for some aspect of starting the business, things wouldn't get done and it would hold me back. It required discipline.

Shifting Passions

By now, Resources was done with formulating my product. They were done with helping me put together the marketing materials, too. On my lunch breaks from the makeup counter, I would go to the Resources offices in Doral Plaza, a high-rise office and residential building on Michigan Avenue, and continue to work at establishing the business. I named my company Michele Foods, Inc., and I incorporated in October 1984.

Before long, my passion was shifting from Mr. Johnson's job. Every time I'd go to work, I'd be thinking, "Okay, I'm selling this lipstick, but my focus is on syrup." I wasn't excited about going to Fashion Fair anymore. I was excited about going to Resources at Doral Plaza. I knew that I still had to make money. I was hustling for Mr. Johnson. I was making a lot of money, but I determined that I was making it for my purposes and not his. But I knew I couldn't be there for very much longer. When you see your passion fading away from one of the tools that is helping you grow, you have to make a shift. Sometimes, the shift is made for you because very seldom do people voluntarily leave money. That's why people keep jobs—especially moonlighting entrepreneurs like I was then.

Even though I was losing interest in Fashion Fair, I was still making huge sales at the makeup counter. I even had plenty of repeat customers. My work attracted Mr. Johnson's attention. He started appreciating these emerging qualities in me. So he came to me and asked me to take on more responsibilities with Fashion Fair. He said, "Since you're doing so well, I'd like you to start teaching skin care in beauty colleges."

He wanted me to start teaching my techniques on a road tour of these schools. A lot of makeup artists and sales associates might have killed for that opportunity. But I had to tell him thanks, but no thanks.

"I can't do it," I said. "I'm starting my own company."

When I said that, he looked at me and said, "You're doing what? You can't work for me and start your own company." He felt that my trying to become a businesswoman was a threat to my performance on his job. He wanted to know, "How're you going to work for me, and you're trying to start a business?"

The answer didn't matter. The fact that I was still making him lots of money didn't matter. He fired me. He called it a conflict of interest, which put me in a situation where I could not draw unemployment for six months, because they had to investigate the conflict of interest claim. So here I was out of a job.

The prospect of having no income was not welcome at all. My gut reaction was to try to save the job. I tried to work out an arrangement. I remember getting on the telephone with the vice president of Fashion Fair and trying to persuade him not to fire me. He said, "I'm sorry. You don't have a job anymore." And that was that for me and Fashion Fair.

Fired

It sure didn't feel this way at the time—and I don't know who said it first, and I am paraphrasing them right now—but it certainly is true that the best thing you can do for an entrepreneur is to fire him or her. So in a twisted way, Mr. Johnson had done me a favor, although at the time I couldn't appreciate it on that level. But if he hadn't let me go, I might still be trying to figure out my strengths. I might still be getting ready.

After the humiliation of being fired, I was not inclined to go back to somebody else's job. I figured it was time to fully devote my energies to my business. I started concentrating on syrup. There was no other game in town for me. I could now apply maximum passion to this. I thought, "If I could sell $5,000 worth of product for Mr. Johnson in a week, and my percentage of that was $500, I can now flip that." I figured I could make $5,000 and pay somebody else $500.

To think this way, I had to ignore the fact that I didn't have any money, and I didn't have anyone I could get money from. I was in debt, and I couldn't borrow any more. My last bit of money came from Mr. Johnson.

My being fired, though, would be my first lesson that you don't need money to start a business. You need the patience, passion, and perseverance to make it happen. I was determined not to give up on my dream. Nevertheless, I was really depressed about being fired. I went home and went downstairs to my mother's basement. I was looking at my future workplace.

SUCCESS INGREDIENT SEVEN

Passion, patience, and perseverance will make up for what you don't have in money—but no amount of money will make up for not having all three Ps.

Chapter Eight

Scraping the Bottom

When you get into a tight place and
everything goes against you, till it
seems as though you could not hang
on a minute longer, never give up
then, for that is just the place and
time that the tide will turn.

—Harriet Beecher Stowe,
author of Uncle Tom's Cabin

FOR MOST COMPANIES, the first five years are the hardest
because you are often putting more into the business than
you're getting back. And that's why it's said that if your business can go five years, you'll probably make it. Because it
takes five years of nothing—of not having anything—to get
your business up and running, where you can even pay yourself. It's almost like renovating a house before you can live in
it. You have to build it into something comfortable and stable.

Here's a concept in your head that you have to develop.
No one around you is handing you money. No one around you

believes in it. No one around you gives a damn—and yet this is your dream. So you have to pull together all of your resources and then some to make it work. And you never have enough to do any of this.

If you start a business, and the first year you make $20,000, you may have already spent $100,000. You've spent that because you had to spend it. And that's what I did. I had to spend more than $150,000 before I even had a product. So I had to make a decision. There I was. I had decided to be an entrepreneur. I'd left my husband. How would I get the money? How would I do this? My first plan was to work. But then I got fired. What would I do now? Quit the business?

My Determination

It's times like these when you have to dig really deep inside and believe in yourself. You have to really believe that you can do this even if no one else has encouragement for you. God helps those who help themselves. People help people who have things. That's what I've found. So, if you have nothing, then a request for help will likely be met with, "I'm not taking care of you. I'm not paying your bills." Maybe if you're somewhere working two or three jobs and your phone gets cut off, someone may feel sorry and say, "Oh, man, I'll lend you the money." But if you're not working a job, people think there's a chance you won't pay them back. That generally seems to be the attitude of people. If they're hard-pressed to help you while you struggle with two or three jobs to make ends meet, then imagine the way they'll scatter when you tell them you're an entrepreneur and that you'll pay them back when the business gets on its feet.

So after I got fired, I knew I wasn't going to get a lot of help from folks. I had to step back and say, "Okay, here we go again. Let's go get in the welfare line." And that meant I had to be a certain kind of poor to get government aid. You had to be qualified. You had to be officially poor.

I needed a decent place to raise my family. I couldn't stay in my mom's attic for much longer. But an entrepreneur wasn't eligible for housing aid. So in order to get help to get housing, I had to become a welfare mom. I had to not have any money to get low-income housing. So I went from, on one end, being an entrepreneur with this great recipe, envisioning herself being on the road to millions, to the reality of being a mom with three kids on welfare.

Psychologically, I never allowed myself to be "the mom with three kids on welfare." I was always the entrepreneur on the way to greatness. When I stood in line waiting for a welfare check, I wasn't a welfare recipient. I was just passing through. It was simply a means to an end. When I accepted that check, this was my state of mind. I thought, "Okay, now I can go home and I can take care of the kids while I build something for our future.'"

I was on welfare for nine months, and the lean times were longer than that. It was a hard time. But it certainly was an eventful time. As hard as I hustled to keep things solidified, they were still threatening to fall apart. Though I had managed to get housing, it wasn't adequate housing. At one point, Keisha had to go live with her dad for a year because I didn't have room for her, and I couldn't take her to school. Sometimes, we were so short on resources that I had to give syrup to the landlord in order to pay my rent. I would tell him, "I've got some syrup. You can give it as gifts for the holidays." And he would come by and get cases and cases of syrup. I would often give away product. I kept cases of it in my trunk, and when I would meet somebody new, I would open my trunk and give him or her a bottle of syrup.

These were definitely lean times for my family. They also could be scary times.

Another Scoop of Upheaval

I remember one incident in which I went to a currency exchange on 103rd and Halsted. It was about 2 P.M. I went in to cash my welfare check. I was always really conscious about it because when I worked for Mr. Johnson I had changed my manner of dressing, and I had bought a little Gucci bag. I had nice clothes. I wasn't dressed like someone who was on welfare. That Gucci bag was one thing I held on to even when I was selling everything else I had to put into the business. It was a reminder of what I wanted to get back to, a symbol of my hope.

After I had cashed the welfare check—I think it was for about $300—I was pretty excited as I left the currency exchange because I now had some money to work with. Some of it was going to pay rent. And I had food stamps to go get food. It was independence for me, so I didn't feel bad about it, because I wasn't leaning on some man. I wasn't saying, "Well, let me go home and smile so he can pay the rent."

And I knew I wasn't going to be here long. So I could see a welfare mom standing in that same line I was standing in and I'd think, "Girl, I won't be here in six months." That was my attitude. I had to think in a way to set myself apart from my circumstances. I could never allow myself to become comfortable with this. I had to see myself as someone else.

But the guys waiting for me that day outside of the currency exchange couldn't have cared less about who I was or who I believed I was going to be. It was 2 P.M., and they were loitering in front of a currency exchange. They probably saw me cash the check and put the money in my purse. I had cash and they knew it.

When I walked out, they tried to rob me. They attempted to snatch my purse. All I could think about was that this was $300—all the money I had in the world. So I fought them. I fought two men! All they left with was a strap off my bag. And believe me, they were pulling very hard. But it's hard to tear up a Gucci bag.

The police came and I went to the hospital. I had sprained my ankle in the struggle. I remember that vividly. It marked a point for me where I knew I had to get away from this manner of living. Those guys were waiting to prey on poor women who may have had no other choices.

This incident really motivated me. I had to keep my visual imagery sharp. I had to see my way out of this lifestyle. I believed then, as I do now, that you must set your sights on the vision. Once you do that, the tools that you need and all of the lessons you must learn are going to come into play. And that was a tool to say to myself, "So, you're an entrepreneur, huh? You think you're a visionary? Whatever!" I knew I was on level A, and that I had to get off of it. Because this is what level A draws; this is what I was in for, cashing a welfare check. I said to myself, "People who are successful with money don't go into currency exchanges to cash checks."

Today, I deal with checks and credit and debit cards. These are safer ways of making transactions. But I was on the level of taking a $300 check to a currency exchange, because I needed cash. I had to say, "You know what? Let me get off this level because I'm not going to stand here and fight guys over $300."

SUCCESS INGREDIENT EIGHT

If you fight with everything you've got, you'll come out on top.

Chapter Nine

Up from the Basement

Both tears and sweat are salty, but
they render a different result. Tears
will get you sympathy; sweat will
get you change.

—*Jesse Jackson, activist, political leader*

MICHELE FOODS, INC., WAS NOW A CORPORATION. We had one flavor of syrup, Honey Crème. Resources had introduced me to a co-packer—a company that could make syrup from the formulated recipe. This co-packer made fruit cakes for Marshall Field's department stores and for other companies. But they also had a liquids plant with vats, and that meant they could work with me.

The co-packer said that I could get a 55-gallon drum of Michele's Honey Crème Syrup delivered to my mom's basement. The drum would cost $350. I found a bottle company in Chicago called Berlin, and I purchased empty bottles with caps from them. I had a supplier to make and send labels to me. So I had bottles, caps, labels, and syrup in my mom's basement. And I would go down there every evening with Keisha, my youngest. She would sit at the table, do her homework, and then I would have her come over and help me to fill bottles with syrup. Christale and Rosalyn were busy with other things, but Keisha was my helper.

Doing It Myself

I made sure everything was sterilized. Then we would get a funnel, and we would fill the bottles. Those were amusing times. Sometimes a bottle would overflow, or a big bubble would come out of the bottle causing the syrup to overflow. Syrup would splat everywhere! We would clean it up and get back to work, trying not to stick to the floor. We successfully filled several cases of product. One case would take up three or four hours.

Once we filled the cases with product, I would seal them and put them to the side. The next day I would get up, put the cases in my car, and take them around to all of the neighborhood grocery stores on the South Side. At that point, I didn't know what to charge for the product. Now, as any M.B.A. knows and I would later learn, attaching the right price is a complicated and important business—not only does a price have to be high enough to get a profit and low enough to be competitive, but it also has to have a quality that appeals to the customer. Some prices just don't sound good to customers.

But I was flying blind. I just came up with a price. I would go into the local grocery stores and ask if I could put the syrup on the shelves.

At that time, I was selling on consignment. If any syrup sold, I would invoice the store; and if none sold, I would go back to get the product. But I really didn't have much of a customer base. No one was going into the stores to buy the syrup.

So I would tell people about it. I told my friends and my family members to spread the word. To create the illusion of demand, I would go in and buy the syrup myself and have my friends and family do the same. For a while that was my business—our going in and buying the syrup ourselves.

But that wasn't enough for me. I made the determination that Michele Foods was going to be a household name—and that one day I would be in thousands of stores across the country. I made that determination on the South Side of Chicago, carrying product into neighborhood stores, two and three cases at a time with my daughters.

My Unconventional Start

Everything I did when I was getting Michele Foods started was unconventional. I didn't know the protocol. This is how I had to do it. I didn't have a customer base big enough to have a production plant making thousands and thousands of cases of syrup. So my choices were few but simple. Since I now had syrup that was properly formulated and a co-packer that could make it in a professional food-manufacturing facility, I was able to get away with hand packing the syrup the way we did. It wasn't according to protocol if you've got a lot, but it's protocol for people sitting at home trying to make a start. When people make things from home—baskets or cookies or whatever—they have to start somewhere. Maybe there is someone out there now making banana pudding, taking it around to small stores. You do what you have to do. You can't do that on a national scale. But this small-scale start was just that for me—a start.

While I built up my presence in neighborhood stores, I continued to face my personal problems. Emotionally, I was struggling. There was being fired to deal with. I had no money, so there was the fear of not being able to take care of my family to deal with. Then there were all of the other things that I had done to get this far with the business. I thought about it a lot. I had to make it all worth what I had gone through and what my daughters had gone through. The thought became like a turning wheel, a motivation for me. I had to peddle my way out of poverty.

Coming Change

After about six months or so of constantly working at it, my product was in several grocery stores—about forty-eight of them, all of them mom-and-pop operations. I would try any and every store. Wherever I would go, I would sell the product. I was never like, "Oh, no! Not good enough for me." I went to Food Exchange. I went to Food Basket. I went to Stony Island Foods. I went to Chatham Foods—all neighborhood stores in Chicago's African-American communities.

I was unique. At that time, there weren't very many African-American-owned food products. When I would go in and request shelf space, no one knew what to say. So no one turned me down. I'd go in myself and put the syrup on the shelves. I'd walk in with a case, and walk out with hope that it would sell.

Thinking Bigger

After six months of selling exclusively to these neighborhood grocers, I decided that I would make an appointment with Jewel Food Stores in Chicago. Once again, though, I was flying blind. I was not very knowledgeable about how to make my approach. All I knew was that you had to have a product that was shelf stable and that you couldn't take a product that you made in your basement further into a grocery chain. This would be different from taking your product into a mom-and-pop store, where the person who owned the store gave his personal approval to allow your product in the store. When you went to a corporation such as Jewel and Dominick's, they would not accept it that way. There was a buying power bigger than just an individual. It was not a forum where you could say, "Mind if I go and put these on the shelves and see if they sell?" That wasn't a decision one person could make. So that was the difference between getting into mom-and-pop stores and getting into grocery chains.

But I was emboldened once again by something that I had read in the newspaper. Jesse Jackson had led picketing in front of Dominick's Finer Foods. They were building a Dominick's on 79th Street on the South Side of Chicago. Jesse Jackson told them, "If you're going to put this Dominick's in a black community, you've got to bring in black products." And at that time, African-Americans weren't making a large variety of grocery store products, so Jesse was picketing for black entrepreneurs who made hair and household cleaning products. He didn't notice me because I was making a food product, and no one even knew who I was.

A Jewel of an Opportunity

But after Jesse had picketed that store, I felt that this was a good time for me to make my move. Anybody who wants to become an entrepreneur can take that as a lesson. Stay on top of what's going on. Read, read, read. It pays off. It helps you to keep a finger on the pulse. You have to always be very aware. Successful people are always in touch with what's going on around them. When opportunity knocks, you have to understand what the knock means. And you have to be ready and able to jump to answer. I understood this, and I was ready. I may not have known the specifics of how to make my move. But I knew that, even though I was outside looking in, there was a movement afoot and I needed to get in on that movement.

So I made an appointment to talk with a buyer and I went out to Jewel Food Stores in Melrose Park, a Chicago suburb, which may as well have been in another state. I borrowed my father's car for the trip. I had never really been off the South Side of Chicago. I had been out of the state of Illinois when I was little and went on summer vacations with my family, but as far as my home state, I had not ventured out into suburbia. And I had never gone into a corporate buying office. So Melrose Park was a challenge for me to find on that day. But I made it.

I arrived with one bottle of syrup. I walked into the office for my appointment, and the lady behind the reception desk asked me if I was there for a job. She tried to send me to personnel. I told her, "No. I'm here to meet with a buyer about my product." She asked, "What's the name of your company?" I said, "Michele Foods and the product's name is Michele's Honey Crème Syrup." She sort of laughed, like it was obvious to her that I was a nobody, and asked, "Who is your salesperson? What broker network are you with?" I wasn't with anyone, and I told her so. I didn't even know what that meant.

But I didn't care what she thought or how she acted. I was there to meet the buyer and get my syrup into Jewel. I went into another office and I sat down finally with the buyer. He was a huge man who must have weighed several hundred pounds, but his name was Mr. Smallman. He told me that he had been the buyer for Jewel Food Stores for thirty-five years, and he had never, ever seen anyone, let alone an African-American woman, walk into his office with a product that she owned. Normally, he was called on by yuppie salesmen and women selling Gerber Baby Food, Cheerios, or some other established product. Most of them worked for major corporations. Mr. Smallman so admired that I was assertive in coming into his office and saying that I had this new product that he said, "You know what? If my grandson likes it, I'll bring it in. Let me take it home."

I gave him the one bottle of syrup that I had come in with, went home, and waited to hear from him. He called me back in a couple of days and said, "My grandson loved it! We are going to put you in Jewel Food Stores."

The first order was for 672 cases of syrup. When I went back to the co-packer with the news, I asked, "How many 55-gallon drums is this going to take?" He said, "Since you have an order from Jewel, we'll do the whole process here." Finally, I was out of the basement.

SUCCESS INGREDIENT NINE

Hard work pays off when you watch for opportunities and have the determination to grab them.

Chapter Ten

Out of the Basement

I have learned over the years that
when one's mind is made up, this
diminishes fear; knowing what must
be done does away with fear.

—*Rosa Parks, activist*

E VERY TIME I TOOK A STEP, I had to learn something new. I
had gone from thinking that I could make a product on the
stove to realizing that I couldn't sell it that way. Then I went
from discovering that the product needed to be formulated and
to getting that taken care of, to packaging the product in my
mom's basement. And now, I had won acceptance into my first
grocery chain. I no longer had to be tucked away with my
daughter relentlessly filling bottles in a basement. But just
because my co-packer had announced that he could take over
packaging the syrup didn't mean that things would suddenly
become easier on my end. Mr. Smallman had declared that my
product was good enough for Jewel, but the truth was it wasn't
quite ready for its move up the food chain, so to speak.

Before I left the meeting with Mr. Smallman, he gave me a bunch of forms to fill out, including one known as a new-item form. The new-item form is something that must be filled out in order for anyone to place a product into a retail chain. The forms are meant to gather facts—pertinent information that the buyer needed to know about the product. Mr. Smallman told me to take the forms with me, fill them out, and return them to him.

He gave me these forms with the assumption that I knew what I was doing. I was too proud to tell him I didn't. I took the forms home with me and pored over them, trying to make sense of them. I was not sure where to begin, or even how, actually.

Swallowed Pride

I took a deep breath. I had come too far into this process to screw it up now. I had to swallow my pride. I called him back. "Mr. Smallman, this is my first big sale," I said. "It's my entrance into a grocery chain the size of Jewel, and I do not know how to fill out these forms." I waited for him to laugh, and he did, but it was a good-natured and knowing laugh, not a ridiculing one. He told me to come back in, and he would assist me. And that's how I learned how to do the forms.

It was an important experience. There are going to be things in business that you do not know, and you have to ask for help right away. If you're too proud, you better hurry up and get over it. You have to do this to move on. What are you going to do? Let it keep you from learning things that you need to know to move forward? Once you ask and get an answer, you learn it and you know it. Because I had to fill out a new-item form for Mr. Smallman, I learned to understand the form and fill it out. Period. When it was time to fill out one for my next chain, I didn't need anyone's help.

Filling out the new-item form was an eye-opener. I had to determine things about my product that I didn't even know mattered. I had to answer such questions as: What are you selling? What size is it? How much does it weigh? How is it packaged? Is it packed twelve to a case? Is it twenty-four to a case? What are the dimensions of the box in which the product is transported? What is the width? The length? How much does a box weigh? How do you stack it? How many do you sell? What's the minimum order that you would sell? What's the maximum? Answering these and many other questions about the syrup led to my devising a fact sheet that I still use today.

The Consequences of Success

Aside from requiring that I provide these facts, the forms provided instruction for getting the product safely into Jewel.

I learned that there were rules for transporting the product. It wasn't like, "Okay, great, bring me a case of the product out of the back of your car." This time out, the syrup had to go through a dock. You had to have an appointment to bring it in. It had to be shrink-wrapped and delivered on a pallet. I didn't even know what a pallet was. I had to pay a transportation company to get the product from the co-packer to the dock.

Before getting there, however, there were other changes that I needed to make to the product to meet the standards. My label was inadequate because it didn't have a UPC code or nutrition facts. I had to research the process of obtaining a UPC code and I had to provide nutrition facts for the label. I learned that there are companies that will analyze and break down the product for nutrition facts. You send them all of your ingredients, and they tell you how much fat is in it, how much cholesterol, how many carbohydrates, etc.

I had to make sure that the syrup was properly sealed so that it was tamper resistant.

Plus I was required to carry product liability insurance to the tune of $2 million. At first that number really scared me. But I asked around and got recommendations for a product liability company, and I'm still with the same company.

In speaking with the insurance agent, I learned that you paid for product liability coverage according to your sales. So if you're not making any money, you have a very low premium. Every year the insurance company audits your sales to determine your premium. At that point, because I hadn't had any great sales figures, I had a very low premium.

All of these requirements, of course, meant I had to come up with more of the green stuff—yet another difference in working the neighborhood grocers circuit. When I was in mom-and-pop stores, it was a very easy process. I could deliver cases in my car. If they asked for one case, I'd deliver one case. All it cost for me to do that was maybe a tank of gas. They didn't care what the weight was because I was carrying it in. They didn't care about a UPC code because these stores weren't scanning back then. They didn't mention anything about nutrition facts or insurance.

But they also didn't tell me to go knocking on Jewel's door. That was my decision. And I had my sights set even higher, so I had to see my way out of these challenges to getting into my first grocery chain. I thought, "You're no longer an entrepreneur with forty-eight mom-and-pop stores, where you're selling out of the trunk of your car on Saturday afternoons. Now you're a businesswoman who is selling to a major retail chain that has throngs of customers coming in the door. It may be more difficult to be here, but it will be worth the effort."

They say anything that's worth anything doesn't come easy. I guess getting into Jewel was one such thing. It cost me money to do business with Jewel, but I considered it one of the hurdles I had to jump.

The Costs of Success

That first order for Jewel eventually cost me $15,000. It took twenty-one days from that meeting with Mr. Smallman to ship out to Jewel. When I accepted the order, I didn't know that it would cost $15,000. Needless to say, I didn't have $15,000. But I wasn't going to let this order go unfilled. So I had to figure out a way to make it work.

I started in with my ever-sharpening sales and reasoning abilities. I thought things out. Now that I was in my first grocery chain, I had to think differently. I had been reading lots of business books in my efforts to establish my business. I had read about the importance of adequate cash flow. I had to come up with some type of payment schedule that was going to allow me to have adequate cash flow. So I worked with Jewel to set terms that would help me to get up and stay up.

In order to get started, I asked Jewel to pay me early, basically. I persuaded them to pay me in ten days after my delivery of the product. In exchange, I offered them a 2 percent discount on the invoice. I persuaded my co-packer and my suppliers that I would pay them in thirty and forty-five days, respectively. So that gave me at least twenty days of cash flow. When Jewel paid me in ten days, then I could pay my packer. If I had done thirty days with my co-packer and thirty days with my suppliers, there wouldn't have been adequate cash flow. And you have to have cash flow in a business. You have to be able to touch your money and hold your money at some point in a business.

You have to set your terms, and then you have to agree to someone else's terms. You have to make sure that between the terms you set and the terms you agree upon, there is a comfortable window of time for you to take care of bills and emergencies until you get the next big order.

Cash flow to an accountant or an M.B.A. may be a lot more complex, but this is how I understood it. At the time, I thought of cash flow as simply some cash flowing through my hands and being there for some period of time. It was a way for me to put checks in the bank long enough for them to clear and cover my bills on time.

In the early days, if you have little to no money, you will wear a lot of hats. It's sometimes very uncomfortable wearing these other hats. You're an entrepreneur, but you haven't had any of the experience it takes to run a business. You haven't had accounting experience. You don't have any money to hire an accountant. You can't hire a bookkeeper yet. You don't have enough money to hire a salesperson. So you have to really wing it the best way you can in trying to stay afloat. I was teaching myself on the fly.

An M.B.A. might not do things this way, but it worked for me. This system has served me well. In fact, I still use it after twenty years. Of course, I hire professionals today, but I run my office on these basics that I figured out with my first order.

SUCCESS INGREDIENT TEN

Sometimes a little success can have a lot of consequences at first—but the education you gain is worth the cost.

Chapter Eleven

Pushing the Boundaries

You have to expect things of yourself
before you can do them.
                    —*Michael Jordan, athlete*

I WAS ABLE TO GET INTO Dominick's soon after getting into
Jewel, which meant I now had 80 percent of the retail
market in the Chicago area. The question became, what do I
do now? I had to concentrate on moving the product off the
shelves. That's when I really started to learn how to sell. And
it was much different from what I did for Mr. Johnson, because
this time it was much more personal, much more relevant.

At that time, Dominick's was owned by the DiMatteos,
and it was still a family-run business. When you went to their
corporate offices in Northbrook, you saw the pictures from
when Dominick DiMatteo started the stores, and when you
met with the buyers, they knew you personally and would try
to help you maximize your efforts. When they decided to do
business with me, they gave me sales advice. They said,
"Michele, here are some ideas for programs you could run.

You could do some in-store demos here, and you can hand out coupons there."

I told Christale, my middle daughter, "Get all of your girlfriends together and we're going to go do some in-store demos." She and her friends liked doing these sorts of things. They liked it because it was something that they had seen other companies—larger food corporations—do. So when Christale got the opportunity to promote our products, she was very excited. This was our syrup, and we were in the store serving it and selling it to potential customers.

Courting Customers

When I sought attention from the market, I had the urge to continue courting the African-American consumer. It seemed natural. After all, that was how I started. So we signed up to do Chicago's Black Expo. Then we started doing Real Men Cook, a Father's Day event in which African-American men cook their specialty dishes and serve them to hungry festival attendants in major cities nationwide to raise money for charities. People would come up to me at these events and say, "Wow, you make syrup! And it's a black-owned company? Well, girl, I'm going to go out and buy this syrup." And I started to see product moving off the shelves in the African-American communities.

But soon I started to feel pent up, bound by limits. I had been able to free myself of the notion that all I could be was a housewife, then that all I could be was a schoolteacher, and then that all I could be was a saleswoman selling someone else's products.

Now the limits were ones I had imposed on myself. Now that I had come this far with the syrup I had to push past other boundaries that were a threat to my success. I was moving product exclusively in the Jewel and Dominick's stores in predominantly black neighborhoods. That's where I thought I belonged. It was a preconceived notion. It was a comfort zone.

One day I thought about it and I said to myself, "Wait a minute. I'm not a *black* syrup. There is nothing ethnic about my product. This isn't just for the African-American consumer." And then one of the buyers confirmed my suspicions. He told me Honey Crème was a general market product. That was the first time I had ever heard the term general market product. But it made sense.

The General Market

A general market product is one that just about anyone would likely buy. My syrup was selling exclusively in black communities because that's the community I was telling about it. I wasn't trying to appeal to anyone else.

Jewel saw my potential around the same time I did. Their buyer said, "Since you're selling so well in the African-American community, why don't we put you into these other stores?" So they put my syrup into all of their stores.

I got Dominick's to place the syrup in other stores, too, which gave me a much wider exposure because Dominick's had a lot more stores in white communities than in black communities. At the time, Dominick's may have had two stores in black communities. So if I wanted to be successful in Dominick's I had to figure out how to sell to the people in Highland Park, a high-income Chicago suburb, and other such areas.

I knew I could not sell to them in the same manner as I had sold to African-Americans. Many African-American consumers were thrilled to meet a black woman who owned a syrup company and would at least try the product for that reason. White consumers most likely wouldn't.

Attracting these other consumers would be difficult for me. Remember, I'm the woman who could hardly find Jewel's headquarters because it was in the suburbs. At the time, the most I could think to do was in-store demonstrations with my daughters. Talk about tossing a pebble at a hulking giant. My competition was huge and formidable. There was them, and then there was me, this lone little syrup in this big, vast category with all of these well-known, gigantic syrup brands. They had brand recognition and had been at this for years.

Until I came along, there hadn't been a new syrup introduced to the category in fifteen years. Fortunately, it wasn't an oversaturated category, so if you were on the shelves in a grocery chain, somebody was going to buy your product. This eventuality was all that I had at that point. So while I prayed for consumers to buy the twelve bottles per store— amounting to one case of product in each store—the big boys moved product three times faster than I could. They were placing three cases of syrup in each store and then they could spend millions of dollars collectively in TV ads to let—rather, *remind*—their customers that they were there. They could entice consumers with coupons in the glossy sales ads in the Sunday newspapers. I could do none of that.

Picking My Battles

I had to figure out how to get the general market consumer to realize that I was on the shelves. Then I had to figure out how to get them to look past established syrups such as Aunt Jemima, Mrs. Butterworth's, Hungry Jack, and Log Cabin—brands put out by companies that spent millions and millions of dollars on marketing and advertising. Michele's Honey Crème Syrup was on the shelves beside these American icon syrups. How could I shake things up in the syrup aisle? I would wrestle with this question for several years to come. This was my challenge with no money for marketing or advertising. I had only faith, perseverance, and a willingness to put up a fight.

That's the thing about entrepreneurs. We will go up against an army with a handgun. But we know it's not about the handgun. I knew that I couldn't go toe to toe with the established brands the way they went at each other. The most I could do was simply keep an eye on them. Watch, listen, and learn.

SUCCESS INGREDIENT ELEVEN

Watch out for the limitations you put on yourself—they can be just as confining as the ones other people put on you.

Chapter Twelve

The Discovery of My Niche

Success is the sweetest revenge.

—*Vanessa Williams, actress, singer*

SINCE I WAS THE NEW SYRUP ON THE BLOCK I decided not to look at Aunt Jemima, Log Cabin, Mrs. Butterworth's, and Hungry Jack as my competition. On some level, of course, they were—we were all selling pancake syrup. But on another level, they weren't exactly. I considered them to be collectively homogeneous. They were all a dark brown, water-based syrup made from similar ingredients.

I decided to concentrate on the difference I brought to the table. I was unique in a number of ways, not the least of which was my price point. It was around $3 when I entered Jewel, which meant that I was a lot higher than the others. Michele's Honey Crème Syrup was made largely with honey, cream, and butter—and there was nothing cheap about that. It was also in an attractive glass bottle, which was part of my brand identity at the time (although, now that my brand identity is well established, I recently switched to plastic after nearly twenty years in glass).

My Strengths

I knew that I brought something special to the syrup aisles. I was doing this for much different reasons than the corporations. I knew I had to find a way to make that mean something. For the corporations, syrup was often a sidekick product. Maybe they made pancake mix and then reasoned they should sop up some additional revenue with a syrup product. Or maybe they were in the food service side working with restaurants and hotels, and they said, "Hey, let's put it in a bottle for consumers; retail is a good margin. We can make money off of it."

So they didn't come to market for the same reasons that I came. I came because I thought this was the best syrup in the world. I knew it was something special. I came because I wanted self-sufficiency, too. I came naively and blindly thinking that was enough. Had I known what I know now about how poor my odds were (how many times have we heard entrepreneurs say that), I probably wouldn't have done it. That I was passionate enough to keep at it despite discouraging odds makes me feel that my product is different, too.

So my entrepreneurship propelled my product as opposed to the typical reasons of corporations—market share, margins, etc. This was about self-sufficiency for me and my family. It was from a recipe that had been in my family for generations. It was about having a passion for something of my choosing.

When I looked at what the other syrups offered and what I offered, I decided that compared to them, I was a gourmet product. That's how I decide to cast my product. There was only one other syrup of distinction, and that was pure maple syrup, which was made by a number of small companies with no brand recognition. Maple syrup sold itself because it was a desired commodity in and of itself.

We had a lot in common. My price point was high; its price point was high. Maple stood out as an exceptional, high-quality item. I wanted to stand beside it as an exceptional, high-quality item. They were making a go of it with little to no advertising, and so could I, I thought. So I began to see pure maple syrup as my truest competition.

Thank God that there are some people—consumers—who want a difference. I'm one of those people as a shopper, so it helped me to understand such a person. I've always been the type of person who buys based on quality.

There might be 100 people buying Aunt Jemima, Mrs. Butterworth's, Log Cabin, and Hungry Jack, and there might be only twenty people buying maple syrup. But I knew that person buying maple syrup was evidently someone who wanted something upscale and different. So I decided to compete with maple syrup and give that person a choice as opposed to trying to compete with the giant brands. I wanted to paint myself in this light.

It's the Dom Perignon of thinking. There are people who buy Cook's champagne, and there are people who buy Dom

Perignon. You'd have to sell numerous bottles of Cook's to equal what'd you make selling just one bottle of Dom Perignon. The price points between my syrup and the others weren't that extreme, but still, I liked the thought of being the Dom Perignon of the syrup aisle as opposed to being a Cook's.

My thinking was a lot like my approach to selling Fashion Fair products for Mr. Johnson. I realized then that I would rather sell a bottle of skin cleanser for $45 instead of trying to sell eight tubes of lipstick. I liked dealing with consumers who didn't fret over buying a high-quality skin care system as opposed to saying, "Just give me the makeup. I can get some skin cleansers from the drug store."

So I cut a path in a different direction that the more established syrups couldn't: gourmet food stores and high-end department stores.

A Gourmet Identity

I went to Neiman Marcus and found a home in its epicurean department, which is their gourmet food section. Here, you might find only three of an item on the shelf. The more upscale the store is, the less they have in inventory. At Sears, you're going to see tons and tons of sweaters and tons and tons of slacks. They're buying low cost and they're selling to that middle-market consumer who is more interested in affordably priced items than in exclusivity. There's faster turnover at Sears, too, because the items are mass produced for large volumes of people. You find lots and lots of the same things. So you wouldn't be surprised to be on the bus or walking home from school or work and see someone else wearing your plaid shirt, your combat boots, or your blue jeans, if you bought it at Sears.

But Neiman Marcus offers something different. If you are a highly paid executive or a millionaire who shops at upper-bracket stores, you're not as likely to see someone else wearing your same clothes or shoes. You may shop at Neiman Marcus or exclusive boutiques where a designer has made just two or three pieces of an item.

I realized that when you go into a 7-Eleven, an Aldi's, or even a Cubs, you don't see pure maple syrup. To carve out the identity for Honey Crème, I wanted to go where the customers for pricier food items go.

When I started off in Neiman Marcus, they would buy just one case for two stores. They would put six bottles in one store and six bottles in another. My first year in, they also put me in their Christmas catalog. They sold my Honey Crème for $7.50 a bottle! It was $5 to buy it and $2.50 for shipping and handling.

But ultimately, I saw that I couldn't make any money here. Neiman Marcus wasn't ordering a lot of product. Plus it finally dawned on me that people didn't come to Neiman Marcus to buy syrup—though some people would if they found it there. I wasn't in the right place. I saw that I needed to concentrate on making it where I already was. I could do better with grocery retailers.

But having been in Neiman Marcus had its purpose. It hadn't been a completely faulty concept. It made me realize that I could still bathe myself in the gourmet light and be competitive in chain grocery stores. Later, when I looked to expand beyond the Midwest, I would pitch my product in the way I saw it: as a high-end product, a competitor to maple syrup.

This is what my selling point would be. So that's where I started from, and I had to stay with that. That ended up being the value of my time at Neiman Marcus. It was only a stage to signal to the buyer that my product had yet another dimension. I would go back and I would tell buyers that we were in Neiman Marcus. They knew I had a quality product if I could do Neiman Marcus.

On top of bringing something upscale, I was bringing retailers something they didn't have yet—a natural competitor for maple syrup. "Your customers deserve another choice on par with maple syrup," I told the buyers. That's how I would eventually persuade some buyers to say, "Okay, great. There's a place for you."

I knew if I could make buyers understand and appreciate this, I would be piling on another plus in the value-added department. I wanted to show them that they got more than they bargained for when they opened their stores to my product.

SUCCESS INGREDIENT TWELVE

Carve out your identity and make it work for you.

Chapter Thirteen

Good Timing

It takes an uncommon amount of
guts to put your dreams on the line,
to hold them up and say, "How
good or how bad am I?" That's
where courage comes in.

—*Erma Bombeck, humorist*

TO THE CONSUMER, my product was for the general
market, and people of all races were starting to choose
my product. But I had approached Jewel emboldened by Jesse
Jackson's picketing of Dominick's to include black-owned
goods. Still, I had not gone into the buyer's office and
demanded, "Let me in or else the pickets come back!" So after
I got in I allowed myself to think for a while that I'd gotten in
because Michele's Honey Crème Syrup was that good. It is a
damned good syrup, and the consumer knew that. But for the
chains themselves, doing business with me was never about
the product. Jewel, and later Dominick's, didn't need another
syrup.

I had come along at the right time. It was the mid-1980s, and Jesse Jackson was talking about affirmative action, and everybody it seems was talking about helping the small company. Where I had thought that they were putting me on the shelves because I had this great syrup, I began to wonder if instead they laughed and thought, "She ain't gonna last. Just put her on the shelf and don't worry about it. It's our duty."

A Diversity Tool

So I was a diversity tool for Dominick's and Jewel. I was someone who they could hold up as an example. I was an African-American woman with a syrup—a general market product, which was very safe. They could reason, "Well, we could put her syrup on the shelf, and no one will know that it's a black-owned product; but we can also tell people that we're doing business with blacks. We can do our diversity thing. So this is great." The consumers that cared whether their grocery store did business with woman- and minority-owned-businesses would continue shopping at Jewel and Dominick's, and the consumers that didn't care would never notice.

They could go to their corporate meetings and say, "Oh, yes, we're doing business with blacks." Or, "We're doing business with this African-American woman who has a syrup." So it was a win-win situation for them.

But I won something, too. I may have felt sometimes as if I were on the outside looking in, but at least I was now doing so from inside huge, brightly lit, and heavily trafficked grocery stores.

I was caught in the midst of a turning point. I knew very little about this big whirlwind—this big tornado—of diversity initiatives that were underway. But I was blessed to be a part of it. Being caught up in those times propelled me further into this business, no matter what the motives of my distributors may have been.

My job from here was to make sure that I built a strong foundation so that they couldn't say, "We gave her a shot, but she blew it." Diversity may have gotten me in the door, where a black woman couldn't have just a few years earlier. But only a high-quality product that pleased my customers could have kept me there.

Staying Connected

Over the years I would learn more about diversity initiatives. *Dollars and Sense* magazine, a magazine that tracks the success stories of African-Americans in business and corporate America, honored me with an award after I had been in business for four years. In 1988, they called and wanted to give me one of their Top 100 Black Professional Businesswomen Awards. That was my first award for my work with my business. Then in 1994, I was also inducted into their Next Level Business and Professional Hall of Fame.

The magazine was more than the source of awards, though. It was a true resource in other ways. Later, at a *Dollars and Sense* magazine conference held in the Bahamas, I met Jesse Jackson. I went on to work with his Operation PUSH Food Spoke, which was developed to help budding entrepreneurs gain access to the retail and foodservice arenas. Plus, when I went to discuss the award with the editors, I met Yvette Moyo, who would later found Marketing Opportunities in Business and Entertainment, better known as MOBE, which provides resources, contacts, and connections for entrepreneurs and corporations. At the time, though, she was working in sales and marketing with *Dollars and Sense* magazine.

We stayed in touch over the years, and I have had the pleasure of watching MOBE grow into quite a force. It has been a tremendous help to minority-owned businesses, my own included. Real Men Cook, MOBE's annual Father's Day festival, has grown to include major cities all over the country. Yvette gave me the opportunity to expose my product to that audience. I also was keynote speaker on MOBE's twelve-city tour one year. I'm proud to be a part of all of this, and in 1993 being a major part of a diversity initiative at a restaurant chain would transform my business again.

The Way It Works

But back in the 1980s, I was concentrating on grocery stores. Grocery stores are in the business of real estate. For the most part, grocers don't own the products they shelve. They rent shelf space out to the manufacturers that do. Whenever a retail product such as mine goes onto a shelf, the grocer assesses a fee. These are called slotting charges. Some manufacturers may pay upwards of $30,000 for their shelf space. On top of the slotting fee, the grocer takes a percentage of the sale of every product—anywhere from 15 to 35 percent. So, of course, grocers are going to be concerned with how an item turns over—or not—because that determines whether they're making money off of it.

Because both Jewel and Dominick's wanted a relationship with me—an African-American and female business owner—they waived the slotting fees. This allowed me to maximize what little resources I had to make a go of it. Letting me in meant sacrifices for them. I imagined them saying, "Okay, we have to weigh the right thing to do with our need to make money. So what we'll do is, we'll just have to sacrifice this little shelf space." So I was just squeezed right on in. It wasn't a scenario like, "Let's knock somebody off the shelf and put Michele's Honey Crème Syrup in their place." I had to stand up next to the bigger companies with all their resources.

Nevertheless, I had been granted a spot. I intended to protect it the best way I could.

Watching My Back

I had to make sure that my product was sitting front and facing center because when I wasn't looking, somebody would come in and just move me out of the way. Unfortunately, sometimes that's what representatives from rival companies would do. They would put me in the back and put other syrups in front of mine. They would do that even if they had four "faces"—four rows of product, lined up, so that the front of their product showed four across—to my one. Having four faces means people can see you. If you only have one, you might be missed. But if I had just that one, I had to protect it and make the best of it.

So I was on a mission. I had to make sure no one encroached on what little I had. Between Jewel and Dominick's, I was in 900 stores. I couldn't just say, "Let me just be content with what I have." No, I wanted more! If I was in 900 stores, I wanted 900 more. And where are these additional stores? I couldn't rest on my laurels.

I started to do my homework, and I would find out startling information such as Aunt Jemima sells $30 million worth of product a year and that they sold a case a day in every store they were in. I wondered how they made that much syrup. I had to really expand my thinking, and then I had to apply my expansion of thought to my product.

But before I could even think of another move to make, the business I already had was threatened.

SUCCESS INGREDIENT THIRTEEN

Be grateful for the good fortune that's given you whatever measure of success you've won thus far—and fight like hell to keep it.

Chapter Fourteen

Eating Bad Product

You gain strength, courage, and
confidence by every experience in
which you really stop to look fear in
the face.

—*Eleanor Roosevelt, first lady*

ONE DAY I GOT AN ALARMING CALL from my co-packer.
There was a major problem with my syrup. He said that
I should come to his office so he could talk with me about it.

When I got there, he said that my syrup was spoiling.
"This product becomes rancid after sixty days," he said.

I was thrown. Of course I had already learned—the hard
way—how important shelf life was, when I had started out
making the syrup on my stove according to the original recipe
and it had spoiled after a day of sitting out unrefrigerated.
I had sold all of my possessions to pay to have it properly—
and professionally, I thought—formulated. So what this man
was saying just didn't make sense to me.

A Terrible Setback

The bottom line was that I was in big trouble. I had to check it out for myself. I went around to different locations for Jewel and Dominick's, and I saw that the syrup had separated in some of the bottles. When I opened one of those bottles, the contents smelled awful. The syrup had become rancid because of the butter in the formula. I thought about all the customers who had Michele's Honey Crème Syrup at home on their shelves. If they hadn't used the product within two months of purchase, it would go bad.

I felt horrible about this. I felt responsible, though this wasn't my fault. I am not a food chemist, so I did not know to ask for something called a stabilizer, an ingredient that would have given the syrup an even longer shelf life. I had asked for a shelf-stable product that I could place in retail stores and assumed that would do it.

Evidently, though, "shelf stable" meant something different to the chemist at the company that formulated my syrup. They probably thought I was going to be here today, gone tomorrow. They thought that I was going to fail. Although the co-packer hadn't formulated the product, they had upset me, too, because I believed that they could have told me sooner that there was the potential for this spoilage to occur.

So I left them that day determined to find another packer.

Clean Up

At a time like this, some people would say, "I've gone as far as I can go. I cannot redo this thing." I just couldn't be one of those people. I went home and prayed again. I would have to have the syrup reformulated. It would cost more money— money that I did not have. I was still struggling. What's new? But I had to figure out how to do this.

The first thing that I had to do was have all remaining product removed from shelves in Jewel and Dominick's and the other stores that individually carried Michele's Honey Crème Syrup, which meant I had to eat the cost of the bad product.

I found a co-packer in Gurnee, Illinois, and that was no small feat. There wasn't a reference book on how to find a co-packer. The company that I turned up was called Kalva Corporation. They were making products for themselves and for large companies. They didn't need to advertise. They were not in the Yellow Pages.

I spoke with a gentleman named Joe LaForge. I started telling him that I had this product that had turned rancid and that I was looking for a co-packer, someone to make it for me. I was quite surprised when he said, "I know what product you're talking about. You're talking about a honey syrup. I saw it on the shelf, and I know your problem."

He told me exactly what was wrong with my formula. And he invited me to come out to Gurnee to talk more about it. So I went out there and saw that Kalva had the facilities and the equipment to make my syrup. I asked Joe what he would put into my product to stabilize it. And he told me about butter buds—butter that has had the fat and water removed and that is then made into a powder. He said it would solve my problem, and the syrup would still have the flavor of butter.

Starting Over

It felt like I was starting over and I had already been in business for a year. I had assured my distributors that I was taking care of the problem, but I was very concerned about getting back in and regaining their trust and respect. Joe assured me that he could save my syrup with a new formula. He said, "I will make it for you. All I need for you to do is supply me with the bottles and the labels."

If it were that simple, I wouldn't have gotten into this mess to begin with. I got more specific in my request this time. "I need for you to give me at least ninety more days of shelf life, longer than that if it's possible," I said. He told me he could make it last a lot longer than that even. So I decided to go with Kalva. Now my product has a shelf life of almost five years.

Loss of Control

There was a price to pay for my newly formulated product—money I didn't have. I had to give up what little control I felt

I had over the company. I wouldn't be able to pay Kalva to reformulate the syrup, make, and bottle it. Plus, I had to order enough bottles, caps, labels, and raw materials to be able to place two to three cases in the chain stores and at least one in the smaller stores. So I needed this co-packer, a company that I was new to, to throw me a lifeline.

We worked out a deal in which I had my receivables signed over to Kalva Corporation.

I told Joe frankly that I was out of money. "So what I'll do is, I'll go get the business. I'll have the distributors send the checks to you. You take your fees off the top, and then you pay me the difference." Kalva agreed and I was back in business. It was scary to give them that control, but I didn't have much of a choice. There was no line of credit or anything like that for me to count on.

Certain that the formula was fixed, I went back to Jewel and Dominick's and the other stores and asked to be put back onto the shelves. I told them about having the product reformulated. They made room for me once more.

SUCCESS INGREDIENT FOURTEEN

Do whatever it takes to recover from a setback, and always keep faith.

Chapter Fifteen

Dreams of Expansion

When one door shuts, a bigger and
better one will always open.

—Cheryl D. Broussard, author of
Sister CEO, *financial advisor*

I WOULD REMAIN A REGIONAL PRODUCT for nine years. The problem with the rancid syrup had become a distant memory, and I had gotten on track enough financially to have my receivables cut to my company once more instead of to Kalva Corporation.

I had gotten into a comfortable groove with Jewel and Dominick's. And I had pressed flesh with a lot of consumers at all the local events I could possibly attend to market the syrup. Everywhere I went I handed out samples. And, of course, there were in-store product demonstrations with my daughters where we made countless pancakes and served them with Michele's Honey Crème Syrup to shoppers in the grocery stores.

But here was the problem: we may have been sticky and caked in pancake batter, but we weren't making any dough that stuck around. And I was growing weary of it.

Stuck in a Rut

I had gotten in because I was an African-American business-woman and because diversity and affirmative action were hot topics. Washington was still talking about equal opportunity for women and small businesses. So all of the different elements that went along with my success were fanning out in all the areas. I was operating on the pulse of that.

But all along I still suspected that I had been put on the shelves for those reasons, but I wasn't expected to succeed. I wasn't expected to sell thousands and thousands of cases of syrup. I was expected to just show up and be there as a diversity fulfillment, as an affirmative action figure and as a woman-owned business. I was just great for the Diversity Checklist, as I call it. After they gave me the opportunity, no one cared that I wasn't making any money. But I cared! I was thinking, "Wait a minute! This is my life, and I'm working hard every day and coming home without a paycheck. It's taking everything that I have just to keep product on the shelves and pay the co-packer, pay the bottle and label suppliers, the transportation company, and everybody else. I can't even hire anybody. I can't buy a car. I can't buy a home. I'm just stuck."

Uncomfortable Comfort Zone

Once while I was at Kalva Corporation on business, I struck up a conversation with Joe LaForge about my dilemma. I said, "Joe, I'm not making any money. All I'm doing is recirculating money. This has got to change for me. How do you make money in this business? How do Aunt Jemima and the others make money?"

Joe told me that the big competitors sold in volume: "They sell their product all over the country, and they sell a lot of product. You've got to get a lot more orders." It was like someone had switched the lights back on after a storm. From his comments, I had my marching orders.

I know how simple and obvious Joe's remarks may seem, but it felt like someone had flashed a shiny object in front of my eyes and suddenly a repressed memory popped up. What he had just said got me to thinking again about how high my dreams had soared before I was brought back to Earth by the rancid syrup disaster. That had taken more than a little wind out of my sails. I had nearly lost everything, and it made me realize I needed to learn this business through and through right there in my own backyard before making another move. Plus, I had scrambled to fix the problem and had to put my pride and possibly the future of the business on the line by having my monies paid over to someone else. After I had made it to the other side of this situation, I had put my expectations on hold and I guess I had just settled into another comfort zone.

Years can go by awfully fast when you get into a comfort zone—even if you're not happy. So I had spent all this time in the Midwest because I knew this region.

I could go to see my product anytime I wanted. I could get up and ride over to the West Side and see it on shelves. Or I could go personally to stores on the North Side. I had friends and family keeping an eye out on product in their neighborhoods. If something was wrong—if it had been pushed to the back of the shelf, for instance—they would fix it for me. They would do this for me out of the goodness of their hearts; now that the dream had come true for me, I had a cheering section. So not only was I feeling cozy where I was, but I also had finally felt a bit validated after years of sacrifice and hard work. I finally had gotten a handle on things enough to prove that I was not crazy to start a business with the family syrup recipe.

Still, it was time to break out of the Midwest cocoon. Once again, though, I hardly knew where to start.

Monday Morning Ritual

I picked up the phone one day in late 1990, and I made the first of what would be a year-and-a-half's worth of Monday morning calls to Flagstar, parent company of Denny's Restaurants. I wanted to do business with them, even though they resisted me from day one. Every time I called, they gave me the runaround. It was very frustrating, but I was determined and all I knew how to do was ask to be considered at the very least.

Then one day I opened the newspaper and I read that Denny's was in hot water with a racial discrimination case against them. It was yet another horrendous episode where an American corporation had denied basic humanity to African-Americans. Among other things, the suit alleged that blacks were being asked to prepay for their meals.

I knew Denny's would finally see me now—they had no choice. I had been calling them for a year and a half every Monday morning at around 10:30. Because they were involved in this high-profile mess, they would need someone like me. Once again, it wouldn't be about the syrup; it would be about a relationship, positive publicity, and photo opportunities.

But I would not let that deter me. I didn't feel as if I needed to throw a tantrum and declare, "Either you take me in because of the quality of my product or I don't want to do business with you!" I would look at this in the same way as I had the Jewel and Dominick's situation. I know that my product is damned good. So the buyers get their relationship with an African-American businesswoman and your customers get the great syrup they deserve.

SUCCESS INGREDIENT FIFTEEN

Opportunity will only knock if you're persistent and motivated.

Chapter Sixteen

Growth

One isn't necessarily born with courage,
but one is born with potential.

—Maya Angelou, writer

IF I WAS GOING TO REALLY GROW MY BUSINESS, I needed a more organized approach to getting business. I needed a business plan yesterday! I started to do my research toward that end. Going to the next level would require cash that I did not have, so I had also begun to think about trying to attract an investor or a partner.

Meanwhile, bit by bit, I was starting to get attention from the local media, and that was helping me to get business. I was accepting invitations to speak about my business and the syrup on small radio stations and the black press was writing feature stories about me. I began to see the magic of media exposure and how it relates directly to sales.

WGN-Channel 9 News called one day and asked me to do a segment with my family about the syrup. Reporter Steve Saunders came out to my home with a camera crew. We had a lot of fun, but it was also a lot of hard work. Before they arrived, my family and I, including my parents—had been up for hours preparing a feast of fried chicken and waffles and a variety of other foods that went well with Michele's Honey Crème Syrup.

The Biggest Store in America

After the segment aired, I got my first real taste of the power of the television media for a small company such as mine. Someone from Wal*Mart saw the segment and called WGN inquiring about me. They spoke with Steve, the reporter who had done the story. Steve called me and told me that Wal*Mart was interested in talking with me about possibly coming into their stores. I was so excited! Before I even called, I knew, they would be my ticket out of the Midwest.

I spoke with the people at Wal*Mart and they told me about a couple of programs that they had in place, programs that could get my syrup onto their shelves. Wal*Mart was a very aggressively growing retail chain, and they had a very diverse set of people coming through their doors to buy a very diverse set of products. The company recognized that all of its customers were not white males and females. With all the talk of diversity, Wal*Mart wasn't going to be the one to take it lightly.

Diversity at Wal*Mart

A guy named Wayne Easterling was the diversity coordinator at Wal*Mart at the time, manager of Wal*Mart's Minority and Women-Owned Businesses Development Section. His job was to go out and find people like me with products that he could groom as Wal*Mart suppliers.

Wal*Mart also was an advocate of American might. They had come up with something called Made In America, a program that supported domestically made products. To get your product into Wal*Mart, it had to be produced in America. That meant that your item had to be composed by American labor with raw materials produced within the United States. This was at a time when Wal*Mart was solidifying its identification. They were growing. They had a plan, and Made In America was a big part of that plan.

Wal*Mart sent me applications for both programs. There wasn't much I had to do to qualify for the diversity program. My company was 100 percent minority owned. The Made In America program was a breeze, too. I passed the test because everything I bought was American produced. I bought corn syrup from ConAgra in Nebraska, butter from a supplier in Wisconsin, honey from farms in Michigan, and the rest of my raw materials domestically as well.

Wal*Mart put me on shelves in some—but not all—of their stores. But they had helped me to attain a goal—expanding out of my comfort zone.

Exploring Options

With the entrée to Wal*Mart, my need for a business plan and for more capital to grow was even more pronounced.

I got some books and took a stab at a rough plan. It showed that I really could use the help of someone who knew a great deal more about these things. But I pressed on and kept trying to fine-tune it myself until I could work out something else.

A friend of mine knew Evander Holyfield personally, and I considered asking for an introduction. At this time, Evander was at the peak of his career. To some people that might have been intimidating. But I wanted to do business with him, and I called my friend and said so. After receiving the go-ahead from Evander's camp, I sent him the rough business plan I had prepared. His office called me back and said that Evander found the business interesting, but they weren't sure what I wanted him to do. Well, I certainly was about to tell them! "I would like to talk to him about investing in Michele Foods," I said. They said that they would speak with him to that end.

When I heard back from Evander, he had decided against backing me. But before I could be too disappointed, there was a silver lining. He didn't want to invest in my company, but he was interested in getting into the food industry with his own product. He didn't know anything about the industry; he didn't even know what product he wanted to put on the market. But he wanted to hire me to help him determine what would be a good fit.

Evander wanted an item that he could market using his name Evander Holyfield—The Real Deal. I was pleasantly surprised by his request. I thought about it, and I decided to take him on.

My mother came with me to Evander's home. We sat and discussed his diet and food preferences with his housekeeper and cook in order to begin the process of developing an appropriate food product with him. We would work off and on with Evander trying to determine just the right product for a few years. But he wasn't focused on this side venture.

Then in the summer of 1997, he had the infamous fight with Mike Tyson where Tyson bit part of Evander's ear off. People started making crude jokes about it. Instead of calling Evander The Real Deal, they called him The Real Meal. So his food industry goals were cooked. It no longer made sense for him. Long before then, though, I had felt him wavering. Even if he had still wanted to do it, he probably could not effectively focus on being in the food business. So I had to let that one go. But Evander has remained a friend and a supporter through the years—my time with him certainly wasn't wasted.

An Investor, Finally

In just about the same period that I started talking to Evander, I met another gentleman who also was a potential investor. A minister who was familiar with my business and wanted to help me introduced us to each other. I worked on the business plan a bit more to prepare for meeting with this other potential investor, who was a Chicago area businessman.

After I went in front of the Chicago businessman and his financial advisors, the businessman decided that he liked the potential of my company. His banker agreed that this would be a good deal for him, and that he should invest in my company.

The businessman had agreed to come in at a capped-off amount. He would invest $150,000, but he wouldn't invest it all at once. It was set up as a line of credit, and as I needed money, he would write checks.

It felt good to know I was easily covered when I needed bottles and caps, labels, or raw materials for Wal*Mart, for instance. He would simply write a check to cover these costs. I would submit a budget to him every month stating how much I had spent, and he would take care of it. If I needed $4,000 that month, it was no problem.

Christale, who at twenty-one was still my right hand, and I kept a log on what I borrowed from the investor. We were careful not to abuse this resource. We knew that it was limited, for one, and that it was meant as a stepping stone to a day when we could comfortably cover our own business expenses, for two, and that we had to pay it back, for three. But it was just wonderful to have support.

Another great part of the deal was that we could move into the investor's office space in LaGrange, Illinois. This gave us the added resource of professional facilities from which to work. Up to this point, Michele Foods had been a home-based business.

We filed paperwork with the investor as to the terms of repaying the borrowed monies. I signed the document, confident that I would soon be in a comfortable position to begin repaying him and to move into my very own office space. It was just a matter of time.

This was a great setup. I had an investor, finally.

I was flying high, alive with the possibilities. But all was not well with me.

SUCCESS INGREDIENT SIXTEEN

Taking any endeavor to the next level is thrilling and demanding.

Chapter Seventeen

One Helluva Headache

I could never say in the morning,
"I have a headache and cannot do
thus and so." Headache or no headache, thus and so had to be done.

—*Eleanor Roosevelt, first lady*

IN LATE 1992, I WOKE UP ONE DAY with the most painful headache I had ever experienced. It eventually faded, but it left me with a sickening feeling, a sort of premonition that it would be back, that it hadn't exactly come out of nowhere. When you experience a headache or any physical pain such as you've never felt before, you aren't likely to blow it off as just an isolated thing.

But I had so much on my plate, and I was moving so fast that I tried to simply ignore it. It would not be denied, of course. It came back here and there. Meanwhile, even though I needed help—and plenty of it—in running the business on a daily basis, I couldn't bring anybody aboard. This time it wasn't simply because I lacked money. I had an investor who would have helped with that. But I was moving fast, I had all of the business' processes and functions in my head, and I didn't think I had time to train somebody to take on what I thought I could handle anyway. It would also mean trusting someone to do it with the care that I would apply to it.

Executive Syndrome

I did have family help. By this time, Christale had come aboard full-time. She became my administrative assistant, my Girl Friday, my bookkeeper, my confidante—my everything. It was baptism by fire for her, too, just as it had been for me, because there were a lot of times when she had to make decisions when I wasn't immediately available. She needed to learn the business from top to bottom—at least as much of it as I knew—and I was trying to teach her on the run. My mother also worked with me occasionally.

All the while, this headache had just gotten terrific. Each one was more vengeful than the last. I woke up with it, took pain killers all day, and then went to sleep with it. Finally, when it just wouldn't go away, no matter how many pain killers I took, I went to my doctor and told her about it. She told me that she suspected that it was a stress-related condition.

My doctor thought I had Executive Syndrome, which she explained struck businessmen running companies. It manifested through headaches and tension. I'm not a white male executive, so I kind of thought it was ridiculous. Even though I was stressed, I loved what I was doing. I was especially excited those days because it seemed to be raining opportunities. I was looking to expand with Wal*Mart. I was working on Evander's recipes. I was closing in on a deal with Denny's, and I was working out a relationship with the investor. At the same time, I was still taking care of the day-to-day operations for Michele Foods.

It was no time for me to have health problems. So I tried to buy into this Executive Syndrome and to keep propping myself up with pain medication. Now that I had the investor and a line of credit to draw from, I was frequently hopping on planes and making sales calls across the nation. I had my eye on Kroger and Winn-Dixie and other grocers in the South. I was determined to concentrate on my desire for expansion.

Then one day I noticed that I couldn't see very well. Gradually, it got worse, so much so that I had to start reading with a magnifying glass. But I pushed forward and tried to look past it—ironically, since I couldn't see! I thought, "I won't be licked by a nagging headache, and so what if I can't see exactly?" I had Christale. As long as she could see, I could see. We worked out a plan whereby she would be my eyes. We would not let any business associates know that I couldn't see and therefore couldn't read.

The plan had some kinks in it. I was in need of a new packer—my third since starting Michele Foods—to solidify the new business with Wal*Mart. I found one in Michigan, but I had to go and meet with them to finalize our relationship, and I couldn't take Christale. I had to catch a plane to Michigan, and then drive about 2½ hours outside of Detroit.

I rented a car, and I drove. Except for God, I was alone. It was a harrowing experience. I was on the road with a map, and a magnifying glass, trying to figure out how to get to this plant. And my head was pounding. I had been putting down Motrin as if it were candy. "God, please help me to get there safely," I prayed.

God was with me. I met with the co-packer and decided to have them make Michele's Honey Crème. The journey had been a success. But my problem was not solved.

A Sweet Deal

Flagstar had cleaned house in the upper ranks of Denny's in order to begin restructuring the company in the wake of the discrimination suits. New president Jim Adamson uncovered the fact that I had been relentlessly pursuing business with Denny's to no avail. He knew the company needed to get back on track, and he asked why there weren't a significant number of minority suppliers servicing the restaurant chain.

The previous procurement executives had insisted that there were none of us to be found—even though I had been banging on the door for a year and a half.

Adamson learned about my constant calling. I'm sure that gave him pause. He asked, "What have you all done with her?" They said, "Well, we've asked her for samples." I had sent them immediately, but it seemed like they were just gathering dust.

Adamson wanted to give me some business. So Denny's called me and said they were serious now. But they needed me to develop a formulation that's would work for them, that would be cost-effective, and that could be transported for a reasonable amount of money. It had to make sense. I had to come to a certain price point.

This was the biggest opportunity that had come my way thus far. And I wasn't going to blow it. I found and hired an industry consultant to formulate a syrup especially for Denny's.

After we got the product properly formulated, we found and constructed deals with some of the largest manufacturers of corn syrup and raw ingredients in the nation. We got good deals with a lot of these suppliers. Then we found and contracted with a co-packer in Texas who would make the product for me, and I would resell it to Denny's. I came in at a satisfactory price point for Denny's, and we signed one of the company's first big deals with a minority-owned firm.

My contract with Denny's was worth $3 million. It turned my company around; it gave me the kind of cash flow that I had only dreamed about.

It was a sweet deal. Denny's paid for all of the raw material, bottles, labels—everything. They paid me to get the product made and delivered to their satisfaction. I aimed to please.

SUCCESS INGREDIENT SEVENTEEN

Sometimes life gives you the worst and the best it has—right at the same time.

Chapter Eighteen

Life Comes to a Head

If you can allow yourself to breathe
into the depth, wonder, beauty,
craziness, and strife—everything
that represents the fullness of your
life—you can live fearlessly.

*—Oprah Winfrey, talk show pioneer, actress,
producer/creator, magazine founder and
editorial director, educator, philanthropist*

THE FALSE COMFORT OF THE IDEA that my health problems
were simply a stress-related syndrome had begun to dis-
sipate. I now accepted that there was something far more
than that going on. I had been to all kinds of doctors. I had
my sinuses checked out for a possible infection. I saw a gynecologist, thinking maybe it was a female-related problem.
I saw an ophthalmologist for my eye problems. I was going
to chiropractors. I had acupuncture. I took herbs. I tried
conventional as well as alternative medicines for the pain.
I hated taking so much pain medication. I knew that stuff

was no good in my body, but there were times when I just could not do anything other than swallow pills and hope for the best.

I tried everything, hoping somebody would discover what was really wrong with me. I was tired of doctors. I was chasing after this thing, but it had eluded both my doctors and me. Of course, I prayed a lot. I fought to remain positive. Through this whole process, I had been going to church regularly and having private meetings with my pastor, who counseled me and prayed with me. No one except my pastor and family knew the extent of the situation. My business investor didn't know. Evander, with whom I was still discussing a business arrangement, didn't know.

A Terrifying Diagnosis

Finally, my primary physician sent me to a headache specialist with offices in Water Tower, a downtown office and shopping complex. I went to his office and described the year of pain that I had suffered. I told him about all of the medication that I was taking to alleviate the pain. He asked if I had ever had an MRI. I told him that I hadn't and that I was horribly scared of the procedure. He examined me and performed a number of tests, and then he told me that I would still have to have an MRI to help him get to the bottom of this thing. He had to see what was in my head. The doctor found an open MRI facility for me on Chicago's North Side. My mother and I drove up and I had the procedure done.

When I returned to the doctor to discuss the results, I was nervous but ready to learn what my next battle would be. He took me into his office. "I've got good news and bad news," he said. He gave me the bad news first. "You have a tumor on your pituitary gland, and it's pushing on your visual nerve and that's what's causing the headaches and sight loss."

I was absolutely stunned. This was essentially a tumor on my brain. The pituitary gland is attached to the base of the brain, and this tumor was attached to my pituitary gland. I couldn't believe it. I hoped that the good news would be that today was April Fool's Day or something. But the good news wasn't enough to absorb the sting.

"The good part is that it's in a good place if you're going to have a tumor," he said. "It's in the front of your head. That means we don't have to go through your head. We can go up through your nose."

There was more bad news. The doctor said that the operation could be complicated because the tumor was so large and had been in my head for such a long time. I wanted a more definitive prognosis. All he would tell me is that basically there was no guarantee. "We don't know what's going to happen after this, but we know we have to take it out," he said.

I pressed him for more. I wanted to hear, "Don't worry, Michele. You'll get this done and you'll be able to live the rest of your life in good health." Instead, the doctor told me it was possible that I might have as little as nine months to live after the surgery. That stopped me cold. I broke down and cried.

The doctor scrambled to get me the best care. At the time, there was a neurosurgeon convention in Chicago, so he couldn't readily pick up the phone and dial a surgeon because the major ones were at this convention. He managed to get through to the head of neurosurgery at Northwestern. He told the neurosurgeon that he had an emergency situation. He needed him to see me. The neurosurgeon agreed to step out of this conference to see me. I went to see him and had all kinds of tests performed on me.

Terrible Timing

I struggled to understand why this was happening. I needed to make sense of it. Why was this happening to me now? Things were finally looking up for Michele Foods. I had signed a $3 million contract with Denny's, the biggest deal yet for my company after nine years of struggle. I had invested my life into Michele Foods. I had sacrificed so much. My girls had sacrificed right along with me.

This year—1993—had promised to be my best. I had done so much to get here. I had divorced my husband, started this product out of my kitchen from my great-great-grandmother's legacy, sold my possessions, gone on welfare, gotten into Jewel and Dominick's, survived rancid product, and answered Wal*Mart's call. And now the Denny's deal would make it all worthwhile and take my firm to another level. My world was a whirling ball of activity and promise.

But I had to stop right then and there. I had no choice. I had to get really spiritual and really focused and figure out why this was happening. I believe that there's a reason behind everything that happens; you just have to seek it out sometimes.

One thing I was not going to do at this junction was crack. I was indeed scared. Terrified. But I had to believe that there was a lesson in this—maybe the mother of all the lessons I'd learned so far—and I had to stick around to benefit from it. As scared as I was, I started reassuring myself, "You're going to come out. You're going to be all right. You're going to get through this. You're going to wake up and you're going to be fine. They're going to get whatever is in your head out of it. You're going to go back to work. You're going to be fine."

SUCCESS INGREDIENT EIGHTEEN

Only faith can carry you through the hardest stuff life can throw at you.

Chapter Nineteen

Gaining Clarity

I learned that courage was not
the absence of fear, but the
triumph over it.

—Nelson Mandela, former president of
South Africa, antiapartheid leader

A s POSITIVE AS I TRIED TO BE, I still had to prepare for a bad
outcome. There were my girls to think about. I thought
about all of the loose threads to my business—to my life.
I still had very little structure. I thought, "If something happens to me, who's going to take over? Who knows where the
bank account is? Who knows anything?" Christale was still
learning the ropes. I did not want to dump a mess into her lap
should I not come out of the surgery. The neurosurgeon
scheduled me for surgery in three days. So there wasn't much
I could do now to fix nine years worth of organized chaos that
only I could decipher.

A Promise

I promised myself and God and my business that once this operation was over, I would get my business in order. I didn't even have life insurance. The thought sickened me. If something happened to me it would have been tragic for my girls. They had been just hanging on a thread after all these years of waiting for me to be successful. And I didn't even have life insurance. I didn't even own a home. I was still living in apartments. So I vowed that once this was done with, I would work as hard on my personal business as I had on my professional business. I would buy a home, build up adequate savings, get properly insured for everything, including getting key-man insurance, structure my business, write the legacy, do the business plan, make sure everything was intact, so if something did happen to me, Michele Foods could go on.

Then I realized that, if nothing else, this would be the lesson to come out of this ordeal. I had to get to a painful, sightless point in my life to realize that I had had my eye on only one sparrow. Now I knew I had to look at the whole flock, the whole thing. I had to rise above this, so that I could do it. If I was going to be a businesswoman, to run a company, to make multimillions, I had know what I was doing in all aspects of my life. And so I vowed that when I came out of the operation, that's what I would do.

A Sight to See

The day I went in for the operation was the scariest I had ever experienced. I was very, very, very scared. My whole family was out in the waiting room. I looked at my daughters.

For a year, Christale had read every contract. She went everywhere I went whenever possible, and that's how she was learning the business. Whatever I had to read, she had to read. It was crash course learning for her. But she was going to learn everything about this business because she had to be my eyes.

Rosalyn had had my first grandchild, Lindsey, about six months before. Here was this brand-new life that I was just being introduced to at the same time as mine hung by a thread.

Keisha was young and in the prime of her life, still working on her education. I thought about how she had worked with me filling those bottles of syrup, helping me to build the business from the ground up.

I really looked at my girls. I looked at my father and my mother, my brothers—everybody—and did not know if I would see them again.

Already I could hardly see them because by now I was legally blind. I hadn't seen much in a year. When I would look at someone, all I could see was the person's frame. I would go to church to pray, and I couldn't see my pastor. I couldn't see him! That really scared me. I could not see anyone's face. If someone approached me, I could only determine who they were by their frame or their hair.

It was all so ironic and sad. Here I was at the peak of my career—the peak of my life! Everything was going great. I was on this ladder up, and I was still climbing my way to the top. I could visualize all the great things at the end of this journey. But I didn't see this coming. It's like I had fixated so much on the top that I missed two or three trick rungs on the ladder. I had been sidetracked by this brain tumor.

Optimism

But I went into the operation very optimistic. It was ridiculously early on a Tuesday morning. I was scheduled for surgery at 5:30. It may sound bizarre and unbelievable to someone who has never gone through anything like this, but after they put me to sleep, I had a real conversation with God. He was sort of up on a mountain, and He just talked to me. He led me to what I needed to do after I came out of this. I felt at peace and reassured. He had been there all along. Every time I would go in for a blood test, go anywhere, I would see someone who had something very spiritual hanging on the wall. It was like He was sending me to His angels. There was always a stranger saying, "I will pray for you." There were spiritual icons all around belonging to other patients or members of the hospital staff. I'd see a little porcelain angel figure sitting in the corner of a room and feel a little more at ease.

One particular day when I went in for a test, I was really, really uptight. A nurse gave me blood. She said, "Girl, God is with you. Let's pray together." She prayed with me. When I came back for my six-week checkup, I couldn't find that woman anywhere. I couldn't find her office. I couldn't find anything. She had lifted me up at one of my lowest moments in the whole ordeal. I still think of her today as one of those little angels come to life.

When I woke up after the operation, I was groggy, but I could see that one of my girlfriends was at my bedside praying for me. Later, I had women from the church there praying for me.

I was up, but I wasn't out of the danger zone. When they removed the tumor, infection spread throughout my body. I was on the phone talking to my daughter, and suddenly I went into convulsions. Doctors rushed to my side. I was given a spinal tap. I had to remain in the hospital for medication and monitoring for several days. My nostril was all packed with gauze, and I was in a medicated fog.

One day I got up from my hospital bed, and I looked out the window. I felt like a big kid looking into a giant storybook with all of these vibrant colors. I realized that through this whole ordeal, I had been colorblind. Everything had been grayish to me. I saw a blue car, a red car, and the sun. I saw greens. I saw browns. I saw a butterfly go by and was astounded. I saw colors that it seemed I had never seen before. It was like I had been given a second chance to see the world.

They wanted me to recuperate for six months. I recuperated for six weeks and returned to work.

Back to Business

A few weeks later, Christale and I were working in the office catching me up on things. I was glad to be back and looking forward to getting some momentum going again. I had a routine after-care appointment scheduled with my doctor in a few days. In the middle of something routine—what, I can't exactly recall—I blinked and all of a sudden, I couldn't see again. It was black. I couldn't see *any*thing. A headache set in right afterward, not one as severe as the ones before, but a headache, still.

Christale called my doctor immediately. "I can't see," I said to him. "What's the problem?"

"Come to the hospital," he said.

It was raining very hard, but Christale helped me into the car and drove me to the hospital. The neurosurgeon saw me immediately. I was frantic. "Is it back?" I asked. He assured me that it would take ten years for the tumor to come back. He didn't know what was wrong. There would have to be more tests. I went to the eye doctor to be tested. He also had no answers. I was supposed to go to another doctor, but I was through with it.

"Christale, just take me back to the office," I said. We got in the car and drove away. As we were driving, I got a call on the car phone. We pulled over, and my doctor was on the phone.

"What happened to you? Where are you? Where are you?" he said.

"I'm not coming back there. I'm not going back through that again," I said.

I hung up, and I took my daughter's hand. We held each other's hand, and we prayed. I talked to God. I said, "This is how you want me to be? I'll accept this, but I'm not going back to those doctors because evidently that was not the problem."

I was really depressed, and Christale drove me home. I got into bed, everything forming a question in my head. What am I going to do? I can't see. My head is hurting. What's going on?

SUCCESS INGREDIENT NINETEEN

Life's worst blows can show you something important.

Chapter Twenty

Healing

The greatest glory in living lies not
in never falling, but in rising every
time we fall.

—*Nelson Mandela, former president of*
South Africa, antiapartheid leader

CHRISTALE WAS MY EYES AGAIN for a few weeks. Then one day my mother called to tell me that she had gotten a phone call from a woman who I had met in the course of looking for cures. This woman lived in California and was a herbologist. She had called my mother to find out how I was doing after the operation. My mother asked, "Do you mind if she calls?" I told her to give her my number.

The herbologist called and I told her about the operation: "I've had this operation, and six weeks later, I think I'm worse off than I was before the operation," I said. "What are your symptoms?" she asked.

"I can't see and my head is starting to hurt again."

"Let me send you something," she said.

I thought about it and was skeptical. At this point, I had just kind of given up. I had felt like I had run a marathon and right as I was getting ready to go to the finish line, someone tripped me. So I lay in the bed struggling to find the will to fight back. I didn't want to tell anybody how hard this was. So I was willing to try almost anything.

"Okay," I said finally. So she overnighted me some herbal pills with a little brochure, and on the bottom of the brochure it said, "From God's Pharmacy." The pills were labeled Brain Formula. She called to see that they arrived and she said, "Just take them." I started taking these pills and resting.

Eventually, I started getting this terrific, heavy amount of mucous that just started swelling up in my nose. It was also in my eyes. My ears were stopped up. I started going to the bathroom, coughing up more mucous. It was unsightly, smelly, awful stuff. One day I blew my nose and something so humongous came out, it scared me to see it. I thought I might have blown half of my brain onto that napkin. But after a few moments, I could see again.

The mucous kept coming. It was like I couldn't blow my nose enough. The more I blew and the more I coughed and the more I choked on this heavy mucous stuff, the better I could see. And my head cleared up and that weekend passed and I could see. I could hear better, too. I didn't have a headache. It felt like my head was ten pounds lighter.

I went to my eye doctor and he said, "We don't know what has happened to you, but you've got 20/20 vision." I have taken these herbal pills ever since then.

The Big Turnaround

I called a girlfriend in Atlanta, and I said, "I need you to go with me to Malibu." We went to meet the woman who had sent the pills to me. We both flew to San Diego, then drove to Malibu. I had never met this woman. Her name was Beatrice. She lived right on the ocean. She came out to the car and met us. I was so happy to meet her.

She explained what she believed had happened to me. She said that the tumor was more likely an abscess on my pituitary gland, and that it grew, hardened, and sat on my visual nerve and gave me headaches. So, basically, I needed to cleanse my head. Beatrice said I was probably the type of person who had developed a lot of mucous and held onto it. We stayed with her a couple of days and listened to her ideas about nutrition, the body, and healthful living.

I left Malibu with a clear head, a bag of herbs, and seriousness about my health—physical as well as spiritual.

Back at home, I met with an enterologist who expressed a really similar opinion about the nature of the "thing" that had been in my head. That was good enough for me. I knew I was through with that part of my life. I knew I had the full lesson.

Cleansed Focus

Successful people have to put their lives in order from top to bottom as well as they possibly can. And there is a particular

ranking that you've got to get right. How important is business success, for instance, if you're not healthy? How important is money if you're not healthy? With my medical ordeal,
God was saying, "Let me give you a raw lesson in life. You
have reached out on faith to develop your family's legacy.
You have had trials and tribulations. But your focus is off. So
let's just clean you up. In cleaning you up, you have to not
only understand what you're doing in business, but you've
also got to understand what you're doing in life. You've got
to understand how to treat people, how to eat well, how to
exercise, and how to be a total person. You cannot receive all
of the blessings that I have for you if you do not heed these
lessons."

This would be the basis of my understanding. That's how
people like Oprah do so well. Look at her transformation. We
saw it in front of our eyes. She's healthy. She understands.
There's a certain responsibility you have to yourself.

How successful can you be if you're someone who is
unhealthy? You can't go to a conference and see that all of the
executive women are out for a run and decide to stay in for a
donut and coffee instead of going along. You cannot connect
with successful people if you're not doing what successful
people do. Understanding that health comes before business
and everything else is a part of the success equation. If you're
not healthy, you cannot perform at your peak. I had to understand this. How appropriate for me that God's message manifested through my brain. It was, "If you want to think with
your head, you better clear your head up."

Finally, I got it.

One for the Books

The year 1993 will go down in history for a lot of things for a lot of people. Some people might recall it as the year of the first attack on the World Trade Center. Or they may recall it as the year of the Waco tragedy. As for me, it was the year that gave me so many things, many of them unexpected blessings. It gave me substantial new business. It gave me insight. It gave me structure. It gave me back my health. I was blessed because in the course of starting my business—going all the way back to 1984, I had not stopped to care for myself. I had not thought about it. I was eating on the run. I was grabbing hamburgers. I would feed my kids and not feed myself. And I never exercised. I don't know if better handling of these things would have prevented the growth in my head, but they were necessary still.

Aside from lack of adequate physical care, I came to realize that I also skirted a lot of emotional issues over the years. And like my health, they wouldn't ultimately be denied.

SUCCESS INGREDIENT TWENTY

Health comes before business and before everything else.

Chapter Twenty-One

Be Still and Be Quiet

Work out your own salvation.
Do not depend on others.

—Buddha Shakyamuni,
founder of Buddhism

I SPENT MY CHILDHOOD as a Catholic because that was what
my parents were. I had always been fascinated by religion
and the questions it raised and answered—or didn't. I, too,
was fascinated by the hope, awe, inspiration, and fear of it.
But with Catholicism, I was mostly preoccupied with the fear
factor. This preoccupation began at a very young age.

I remember riding my bicycle with a childhood friend,
who also rode her bicycle. She hit a bump in the pavement,
tumbled from her bike, and broke her leg. I was traumatized
by the whole incident, and began to question why it happened to her and not me. Had she done something wrong?
This was sort of a silly possibility even to me back then, even
as I posed the question. We were so young. What wrong
could she have done at that time to deserve such a thing?

119

My Own Path

Over the years, I grew tired of quaking in the wake of a systematic belief. Intuitively, I did not believe that I needed to be in fear all the time to draw blessings and to stay in line. But I needed to believe in something. I think we all need a well, a place from which to draw spiritual reinforcement. So I would keep seeking until I found answers that made more sense to me personally. I was no longer interested in the system that had been handed to me. Many of us are handed a belief system as we are being raised. It's part of the syllabus of child rearing 101. Parents give their children food, shelter, clothing, and a sense of right and wrong. Often that sense of right and wrong is drawn from a religion of some sort—the one to which our parents subscribe.

I believe that when you become a grownup, you have every right to broaden—or even narrow—your belief system. It does not mean that your parents led you astray. It likely means that they simply did the best they could with the resources that they had—spiritual sustenance included. But as you seek your own way in the world, you could end up discovering that you find spiritual resonance and edification elsewhere. This is what ended up happening to me.

After spending my youth and young adulthood bound by the tenets of Catholicism, I began a search for other ideas to explore my spiritual side. It was a search that ultimately led me to a source of theoretical and spiritual sustenance from which I continue to draw in both my personal life and in running Michele Foods: Buddhism.

I started searching for spiritual grounding during the final stages of my marriage. It started by simply reading as much as I could of anything that encouraged positive thinking. I read and read and read. And it bolstered my sense of self.

One day, one of my best girlfriends in Chicago shared with me her enthusiasm for a "new" philosophy that she had discovered—Buddhism. She described how Buddhism used chanting as a tool for relaxation and spiritual insight. I liked what I was learning from her about it, and began a quest to learn more.

Buddhism introduced me to the concept of cause and effect and to the notion that what goes around comes around. I was intrigued and encouraged by these aspects of this belief system. It was empowering to believe that what you put out you get back.

The aspects of Buddhism that resonate with me most have to do with self-actualization, self-transformation, and self-transcendence. A major quality that I cultivated from Buddhism was the ability to be still and be quiet. I learned the centering effect of meditation, for one. The powers of meditation can go well beyond the moment, too. Long after you've meditated, you will benefit from its residual effects.

Spiritual Business

In business, the ability to rummage through the many inner "noises" that compete for your attention on a daily basis is golden. Recently, I was faced with a mistake that might've been rather costly for my business. I had made a decision to distribute Michele's line of syrups in a large retail chain in the South. We devised a campaign to launch the distribution during Black History Month. I agreed to a six-week promotion.

The store overbought inventory, and unilaterally decided to run the promotion all year—without consulting me. The bottom line is it would cost me $80,000, according to my accountant.

This was terrible, potentially enraging news. It could have sent my company into something of a tailspin.

But I refused to let myself get to the boiling point over it. I said, "You know what? I'm giving this to God. When I get up tomorrow morning, this is going to be resolved in my favor. Period." I didn't think any more about it. And sure enough the retailer's management busted their behinds trying to resolve it. That was how I handled it. If I had been attached to somebody else's fears and insecurities, then I might have reacted differently. But if you know within yourself that it's going to be okay, chances are that it will be. Despite everything I've been through, I've been okay. And I've come through astronomical stuff. But I've always had spiritual sustenance.

I believe that everyone must feed himself or herself spiritually. It takes ongoing cultivation to keep yourself fed, however. Just as your house, your car, your hair, your clothing—just about everything—requires maintenance, so does your spirituality and the many aspects of it.

SUCCESS INGREDIENT TWENTY-ONE

Everyone must feed himself or herself spiritually.

Chapter Twenty-Two

Limited Expectations

When people keep telling you that
you can't do a thing, you kind of
like to try it.

—Margaret Fuller, author, activist

I STARTED MY BUSINESS when I was in my very early thirties, after I had held less than a handful of other jobs—all of them part-time. So I didn't tussle long with the expectations of the dreaded "boss man." The expectations that I fought with were a lot more intimidating. They were of the family nature. Family drama can feel like a second skin that we have to pierce and shed. A lot of our hang-ups can be traced back to when we were kids.

Every one of us—you, me, the Rockefellers and the Oprahs of the world—comes up first as someone's child, someone's daughter, someone's son, someone's brother, someone's sister, someone's cousin, or someone's friend. And when you come up in that environment, you tend to look at yourself first and foremost through other people. What do they do? What do they value? What do they think about you?

When I was a child, I had natural urges that ran counter to how people saw me. I wanted to run and play. I wanted to have fun! But I was the only little girl in a family of five—me; my mother; father; and two brothers, one older and one younger. So I was encouraged to be dainty.

My mother always used to make me get dressed up and sit down on the porch. She'd say, "Don't play because I don't want you to get dirty." All the while, I wanted to climb trees, but I couldn't do it because I was supposed to sit there.

Naturally Competitive

I remember that I was naturally competitive and aggressive. I remember an incident with a neighborhood girl named Phyllis when I was nine. We were growing up together, and I considered her a friend. I even still have a picture of us. One day though, I felt threatened by Phyllis. My mother was pregnant at that time with my youngest brother. It was Easter, and I was all dressed up and my mother was giving this other little girl more attention than me, and I didn't like it. I started to complain about it, to let my mama know how I felt. And my mother was like, "Be nice, don't hurt her feelings."

So I did as I was told.

I went along with the program because everybody went along with the program. You go along with the program because when you come into this world, your parents are the most influential people in your life. So you want to please them. Your parents say to you: "You need to go to school and get good grades. Make sure you get all A's so you can go to a good college and so you can get a good job." And if we're "good" kids, this is what we do.

Passing It On

I see history repeating itself with my granddaughter, Lindsey. We're all giving her behavior instructions and hints about who we believe she is. When she comes to Grandma's House, she often hears: "You've got to be good, Lindsey." "You've got to sit over here, Lindsey." "Don't do that, Lindsey." "Brush your teeth after you eat, Lindsey." "Don't mess your hair; we're getting ready to go out, Lindsey."

At home, she hears from her mother, Rosalyn: "Lindsey, where are your A's?"—B's are not good enough—or "Lindsey, you can't have that."

This is all part of the program. Beyond being told what to do all the time, as children we take cues from what our parents say to us.

One day I said to Lindsey, "I'm going to give you some money for walking the dog."

But her mother said, "She can't have any money."

"Why?" I asked.

"Because she went to school and someone stole it."

And Lindsey's just absorbing all of this like a sponge. She could be saying to herself, "Oh, I'm not responsible."

My point is that we internalize things as children. And some of us, unless we go through some kind of realization, we are those things for our lifetime. Of course, it's important to protect our children and teach them what we think is right. I'm hoping that things will be a little different for Lindsey than they were for me. We might unintentionally send her some confusing messages about herself. But, on the other hand, we send her some definitely positive messages and give her great examples.

At nine years old, for instance, she's got a syrup with her name on it. Miss Lindsey's, one of my products, is named after her. She went to school one day, and one of her assignments was to do a report on an inventor. I was the inventor. So she was able to walk through school and say, "My grandmother's an inventor. I was on CNN with her, and this is my syrup." She's also been in *People* magazine with me, and she always gets the limelight, being the only grandchild.

That's a whole different place for a nine year old than where I was at her age. Her point of reference for her life at nine years old is also different from someone else's who's maybe living on welfare in the Cabrini Green housing project. She may come up and have an understanding about business because she sees it. She sees that her grandmama is in *Essence* and *Fortune* magazines. Her grandmama was on *Oprah,* and when we went to Disney World, and Minnie Mouse had seen me on the show, it was the thrill of Lindsey's life.

When you have this kind of environment, you can evolve differently and at an earlier rate. But that doesn't always ensure that you will make positive choices. It's still always up to you.

The Peach on the Apple Tree

Some people remain enslaved by the examples that they see around them. If they lacked role models, then they find it difficult to grow beyond a certain point. They can see few possibilities for themselves beyond what they see. But you have to stretch.

What's the saying? The apple doesn't fall very far from the tree? Well, I was a peach on an apple tree to begin with. My father was a butcher. My mother worked for the post office. Today they are both in their late eighties. They came of age with much different values and possibilities than mine would be. The way I came of age is much different from the way my girls came of age, and so it will be with my grandchildren as they come of age. So when you learn at the knee of someone from a different generation, you have to make the necessary adjustments in order to make certain moves in life. These are the adjustments I had to make after being reared by my parents. When they were a young married couple, their dream was to raise their children, send them to school, and retire. And that's what they've done. That's what they believed in. They wanted their children to go to church, do well in school, get good jobs, and marry well. I did all of that for a while. But my thing was, I wanted to have a business. So that is what I eventually went after. It was not how I was raised. It's how I took some things from how I was raised and turned them into something useful.

Against the Family Tide

One of the most trying and painful times in this whole journey with Michele Foods was when I had a legal fight with my own family for the right to use the recipe as the basis for the business. It was basically a huge misunderstanding. My mother and brother sued me to try to stop me from moving forward with the business using the recipe. It wasn't about money. It wasn't about control. It was about protecting the legacy from harm that they thought would come to it in my hands.

You have to realize that my parents and my family had never been in the food industry. We were just laypeople, just regular people who had regular, working-class jobs. So in my breaking away from the norm and trying to start a business, no one understood or believed that I was going to be able to pull it off. They believed that if I tried I would just open myself up for failure, rejection, disappointment, and pain. Worse, they believed that I was putting the recipe in jeopardy. They didn't understand that I could protect the recipe with confidentiality agreements to ensure that whoever was exposed to the formulation of the recipe could not tell anyone. Because they did not fully understand, they tried to stop me legally.

There had been a lot of tension between us because their first feelings were, "Michele has lost her mind. She's gotten a divorce, quit her job, and she's in the basement making syrup." So that was their initial attitude. With hindsight, I can understand how they felt. I guess I'm glad that I couldn't see it their way back then. I was very stubborn and very head-strong, and I was really adamant about bypassing them and pressing on.

My brother had lent me start-up money, so of course, he felt that he should have some say. And he did, to some degree. But he didn't fully share my vision. So I moved past him as well. Even though I had wanted my family to be involved in it, it wasn't their dream. I had this vision, and other people weren't seeing it. And when it comes to family, everyone thinks they know exactly what their kinfolk are capable of doing or not doing. They think that because they share your blood and upbringing that they know the outcome of your moves. They rationalize, "Well, you've done a lot of things before and they didn't work out." I had made decisions other people wouldn't dare to make. So a lot of the things that I did, my family did not agree with, but that was all about my entrepreneurial trip. I took chances that they were indirectly forced to take with me on some level.

Say, for instance, I borrowed the money from my brother and had taken the recipe and started this business, and someone else got the recipe and gave it to some corporate food giant that made the syrup without me to the tune of millions of dollars. Then yes, it would have been a terrible situation. That is the only vision that my family had. They hardly heard me say, "I'm going to learn how to protect this. I'm not going to give it away." They asked over and over, "Who are you to do this? Who are you to pull this off?" They didn't think that getting a divorce, selling everything I owned, quitting good jobs, moving back home to the attic really suggested I was reliable or responsible. "Why should we feel that you're going to pull this one off? Before you damage the recipe and damage the legacy, we're going to try to stop you."

So we had some conflict. That is a very painful time in our family history, but it has made us stronger. We have overcome those days and are closer now than ever.

Every situation is what you make of it. I saw Tiger Woods on a TV program hitting a golf ball at two years old. He had met Bob Hope and was swinging a golf club. His father was right there with him. But if Tiger didn't want to play golf, if he hadn't developed a passion, he probably wouldn't still be doing it.

But you can still expose someone to positive things, and they can turn around and be like the Menendez brothers. They grew up rich, but they made negative decisions. There may have been psychological abuse, but they still made the poorest decision when they decided to murder their parents.

So just as somebody can seem to have everything and mess it up, somebody could appear to have nothing and fix it up. It really does come down to the choices we make. It's just amazing to me that a lot of people cannot see this in their lives, that they don't understand that they control their own destinies. I understood that I did, even when those closest to me didn't want to accompany me where I was trying desperately to go.

SUCCESS INGREDIENT TWENTY-TWO

Never let other people's expectations get in the way of your own expectations for yourself.

Chapter Twenty-Three

A Fateful Journey

We are not human beings on a spiritual journey. We are spiritual beings on a human journey.

—Steven R. Covey, author, executive mentor

YOU ABSOLUTELY HAVE TO STRETCH. That's not to say that you can blink and—poof!—all your childhood issues are gone. I think we fight them all our lives. You just have to recognize the source of your behavior. And then it's up to you to change.

I know it's not easy to change. It's hard to change being submissive. It's hard to change being preachy. It's hard to change being co-dependent. It's hard to change being a gossip.

It's hard to change being judgmental. I know this firsthand.

Women at the Top

A few years ago, my good friend Pat, who is the Chief Diversity Officer for McDonald's, joined me and my daughter

Christale on a retreat to Anguilla. It was called "Women at the Top," and it was a summit called for a group of handpicked women who had to be of a certain income and a certain this and a certain that. We all headed to this island where we would have Iyanla Vanzant as a key speaker. We were going to have a secluded dinner with her. As we were on our way to Anguilla, I said to my friend, "Pat, you know what? I really want to stop being judgmental. I'm very judgmental. I don't want to be judgmental."

And as soon as I said that, it seems, everybody around me was somebody I just had to judge. And that's a lesson. Once you put it out there, get ready to back it up. But before I could do that, I needed to come to terms with where the behavior comes from in the first place.

Mine is a really humorous family. I have brothers, and we're always cracking on each other. You know, like, "Look at her. God, what has she got on?" It was always supposed to be all in fun. But it got to the point where it was just judgmental. I got to where I wouldn't want to sit next to someone. If someone sat next to me at the airport, I might think, "God, this is a huge person."

But I knew it was time for me to grow out of this.

By the time the dinner with Iyanla came along, we had been in Anguilla for a couple of days. We gathered in this villa where Iyanla would address us. Pat, my daughter, and I sat near the front. Iyanla started in asking people different things and they would come before the room to speak. She could only take about five or six people, and those were from the people inside that room. There was an overflow crowd of listeners out on a nearby patio. To this day, I know that the people who were in that room were supposed to be there. It was one of those spiritual things. The people who weren't going to get the lesson were out on the beach somewhere. The people who were going to get the lesson were there to get it. I was there, and for some reason I stood up and I started talking. So Iyanla told me to close my eyes.

A Powerful Discovery

"Now go deep inside," Iyanla said. So I went deep inside. I wound up at the age of about nine years old.

"You know, I never felt I was pretty," I said, my eyes jammed shut. "Because I never was told that. I never felt really loved. Because I grew up in a family of real . . . I grew up in a strange . . . " The words would not come to me easily. I caught my breath. "I grew up with a father whose mother was white," I said. "My mother was a pretty brown complexion. So she and I were the only people with brown complexions in my family. I grew up in an environment where internally, I felt different, but it wasn't something we talked about."

Much of what I would say would be freeform. It was all so jumbled up inside. But I started to realize that being judgmental started with myself.

"My mother's mother was brown," I said. "And then I had a younger brother that came along who was favored because he was the baby. . . . So there was a lot of stuff growing up."

I linked these childhood disappointments to my adult self. "I don't feel successful because I've almost never been told I was successful," I said. "My dad *always* believed in me, but no one else that meant anything to me ever said I was successful. When I started this business, everybody said, 'Aw, you ain't gonna do that' or 'You can't do that.' There was never any encouragement, except from my father. I felt that whatever I did, no one else in my family really felt that I was a success. Only my dad walked up to me and said, 'You know what, I'm really proud of you.'" As time went on, people's opinions changed and my whole family was supportive, but at the beginning, it was really tough.

I spoke about how the success of the syrup and Michele Foods, Inc., drew some of my people to me for all of the wrong reasons—and some for all the right reasons.

I told Iyanla, and this roomful of high-powered women that, even at this point in time, I still didn't feel successful. And I still didn't feel pretty. Iyanla had taken me through this process of going really deep inside. I had my eyes closed, and then all of this just came up. And I just cried and cried. She told everybody, "Do not touch her! Do not touch her! Let her cry." And I released it.

After that, I got so violently sick that I literally had to be carried home from the island. I wasn't surprised that she was able to pull this stuff out of me. People such as Iyanla Vanzant and Oprah Winfrey have elevated themselves to a point of understanding. I had released these feelings in a very public way, but that is what made it so liberating. They were my feelings to do with what I willed.

It helped me in my struggle to combat my judgmental tendencies, to understand that it all started with not feeling loved myself. It also helped put me on the road to healing and forgiveness with my family. I believe that I judged the world because I had first been judged harshly by my very own people.

Make the Choice

Rebounding from childhood trauma can be tricky, but I'm glad to say it's possible. You can be left of center of *expectation* as opposed to left of center of *true self*. It's a matter of attaching ourselves to the notion that we can be something else. If you want to become a skydiver, you would attach yourself to that. That would be your desire. I don't have a desire to be a skydiver, but someone else is out there right now on a cliff, getting ready to jump because that's her desire. And her mama and daddy probably didn't say to her, "When you grow up, I want you to be a skydiver."

Your conscious mind is like the captain of a ship. Your subconscious mind is like a ship. The captain takes you where you want to go and the subconscious follows. So if you constantly tell your subconscious mind that you are rich, rich, rich, you draw that to you because your subconscious mind follows your conscious mind to the point of believing what you believe. If you constantly say, "I'm not going to be judgmental," for instance, you reinforce that goal.

You write your own destiny. You control your own destiny. I could get up from my desk right now and walk outside of my office, go across the street, and hold up the gas station. I can blame it on not feeling pretty or loved enough as a child. Or I can continue to build and improve the business I've built from the ground up.

SUCCESS INGREDIENT TWENTY-THREE

You control your own destiny.

Chapter Twenty-Four

Moving Forward

If we have the courage and
tenacity of our forebears, who
stood firmly like a rock against
the lash of slavery, we shall find
a way to do for our day what
they did for theirs.

—*Mary McLeod Bethune, educator,
organizer, political activist*

AFTER MY MEDICAL CRISIS was securely behind me, I got
back to the drawing board, concentrating on the Denny's
opportunity.

It's a horrible irony that for many small businesses, the
very thing that can put us out of business is the new business
that we so desperately crave. If you land an account that
requires more cash flow than you have readily available to put
the account into play, then you can crash and burn.

I had to make sure that if we shot for something, I could come back and figure out how to do it. We shot for Denny's very aggressively. Then I got Denny's, and I had to figure out how to make it work. I didn't own a plant. I didn't have the resources to make thousands of cases of syrup a year for Denny's. I didn't have a staff for that. I had only Christale and me. So I sat down and I figured out a way to work the Denny's deal to bring profit to Michele Foods as opposed to saying, "I can't do that. I don't have a plant." I hired a consultant and together we came up with a game plan.

My strategy has always been to get the business first, especially when it's ripe for the picking, and then figure out how to make it work. I wouldn't be the first entrepreneur to approach growth this way. If you sit back and say, "Well, I don't have a plant. I don't have this and I don't have that. So I'd better not even go for it," you'll never get bigger business. It's just like figuring out what comes first, the chicken or the egg. You've got to know that the egg comes first, then you've got to warm it up so that you can hatch it. You can't stay put in a dilemma. You have to pick the choice for growth. You know that you need new accounts to grow. Then get the accounts and work them. I'm not saying be deceptive. I'm saying have the gumption to get things done.

With the Denny's deal, I figured out a way to bring in about $300,000 into my company without owning a plant, making, or transporting the syrup. I would hire a co-packer that would make the syrup. I would pay the co-packer for his services and then I would resell to Denny's. Michele Foods would profit $1 on every case.

Value-Added Rewards

Because I am African-American, Denny's got a value-added component by doing business with me, but I got something extra out of the deal, too. The Denny's deal gave me entrée into the foodservice industry, which was another facet of the food industry filled with opportunities for Michele Foods. The foodservice industry is much different from the grocery retail business. It's more of a business-to-business model. You are a supplier to such businesses as restaurants and hotels. They are going to buy predetermined amounts of your goods. You are not at the mercy of the consumer. When grocers buy your product, they will buy as much as they are comfortable projecting that consumers will buy within a certain amount of time. When that supply dwindles from the shelves, then they'll put in another purchase order for more product. They advertise and market to get products into consumer's hands, and as the producer of a product in their stores, you also try to encourage consumers through promotions, advertising, public relation, and marketing efforts.

On the foodservice side, if you sell syrup to a Denny's or to IHOP or to the Marriott hotels, you are contracted to simply make the product and deliver it satisfactorily. They will give you a contract specifying something such as "We have 1,000 restaurants. We buy 10,000 cases of syrup a year. This is how much we're going to buy from you. We're going to buy $3 million worth of product from you for a year. Here is how we expect it to be delivered to us."

You don't have to fret over labeling and advertising and marketing and PR. None of that.

Food service is a great part of my business, and I joined the Women's Foodservice Forum in 1997. In 2002, I was given the first annual Entrepreneur of the Year Award, which "recognizes a woman owner, founder or franchisee of a foodservice operation who has successfully grown her business and, at the same time, has developed women leaders and given back to the foodservice industry."

Positive Press for All

I was able to piggyback on Denny's advertising and publicity. Denny's was hungry for positive press on the heels of the discrimination lawsuits and settlements. They featured me in a print ad campaign. They invited me to speak at industry events about my experiences working with them. Their PR machine made sure to trumpet the relationship that they now had with Michele Foods. Through their efforts, I was now landing national press placement. I wound up in *Fortune* magazine. I was in the *Wall Street Journal*. Reporters from all over the country would call and ask, "I heard that you're doing syrup. How'd you do it?" I would start off by saying, "Well, it was my great-great-grandma's recipe." Eventually, the legacy became the focus more than the syrup. It was a human interest story to people nationally now.

The Goal Reached

With it being my style to go out and get the deals and then figure out how to make them work, it was fitting that I had been so determined to find an investor, especially after I had gotten into Wal*Mart. I knew that other larger, more lucrative opportunities were right behind it. If I wasn't ready, I might have to turn down an account, or worse, take it on and fail to deliver.

By the time we were nearing max-out on the line of credit that had been extended by my investor, I was nearing a point where I could make a go of it without any more borrowed funds. The support the investor had given me gave Michele Foods just the momentum it needed to get into a groove with the new business from Denny's, which was a good thing, too.

I felt that I would be ready soon to march into his office with a smile and the announcement that we had reached our goal of being stable enough to manage the business that we had at hand. I thought since the relationship had worked out so well that if we needed to borrow from him again, we could do so for future growth.

But there would be no future between Michele Foods and this particular businessman. He was not what he appeared to be.

SUCCESS INGREDIENT TWENTY-FOUR

Take risks to reach your goals.

Chapter Twenty-Five

Betrayal

I now realize that true success is
always a work in progress.
               —*Cathy Hughes, entrepreneur*

A GROUP OF M.B.A. STUDENTS at Northwestern University's Kellogg School of Management had heard about
my company and decided to find out if I might be interested
in sharing my business story as a learning tool for them.
When they learned that I did not have an official business
plan—there was the one I had done, but that wasn't up to
par exactly—they asked if they could do one for me as sort of
a case study. Knowing what I know about the caliber of businessmen and women that Kellogg turns out, I was happy to
be a subject of interest. I could help them learn something
and they could teach me something by way of their work on
the business plan. Plus, I would have a better plan than I
could do myself.

The students started researching the business. I invited
them out to the office that I shared with my investor so they

could see our operation firsthand. I also went to Northwestern and met with the dean of the business school.

When the students needed financial documentation, I went to the investor to gather them from him. Because he was lending money, I had agreed for his controller to have full access to all financial information. So they had a large portion of my financial documents at this time. I got the materials and shared them with the M.B.A. students. They came back to me later and said, "Michele, this does not make sense." I had told them basically what my arrangement was with my investor and from their vantage point, there was something funny going on. I thought for sure that more complete documents would clear up the matter.

So, of course, I went back to get them. The controller and my investor started giving me the runaround, and kept promising to give me the correct information. But that information never came. The bottom line is that he had played me for a fool.

Business Jacking

What the students had found was indeed the correct information. On the books, instead of documentation that he had lent me $150,000, he had indicated that he had invested $350,000! He hadn't given me that much. There would be no business plan. I had to tell the M.B.A. students to move on to another subject. Although I'm sure it would have been a lot more fascinating and a lot more dramatic of a learning experience, I had to bow out and figure out what in God's name was going on with my company.

Things got to be really weird really fast when I confronted him about it. I was extremely upset when he couldn't give me an explanation that put him in a better light. I told him that I didn't trust him anymore and that I was leaving.

He said, "Well, you can't because I own your company."

When I examined the agreement with the attorney, I saw how I had gone wrong. But I didn't need to see it spelled out in the contract. I knew from the moment I saw the $350,000 in the books that the investor had misled me and that I had gone wrong because I was gullible. I was naive. I was too trusting. Talk about a paper cut! I had signed an agreement that basically was slicing my business right out of my hand. The investor and his highly paid lawyers had worded the contract so that he owned 100 percent of my company until I paid him back the $150,000 plus interest—exorbitant interest.

I couldn't believe it; the investor owned my company for all practical purposes. In order for me to get it back, I would have to pay him $150,000 in cash plus this huge amount of interest. I was doing a lot better financially with the company, but I did not have a way to get him that amount of cash to end this deal.

On Our Own

The day the investor told me that Michele Foods was actually his company and not mine, Christale and I packed all of our stuff and left his offices. We moved into our own offices in Calumet City, Illinois. It was now just the two of us again.

It was disorienting to be back on my own financially, I must admit. Things had changed a lot in the short time that I was with the investor. I had bought my first house and moved in. When I went through my medical crisis, he held things together with Christale. I felt confident that my business was being taken care of while I was having surgery and later recuperating. I didn't have to worry about not fulfilling a purchase order. I could buy adequate raw materials. I didn't have to worry about not having a paycheck, either. I could draw from the line of credit to pay myself and to pay Christale when receivables were slow. This setup had been my security.

Now, regardless of the fact that the investor had not been honest with me, I had to either find a way to pay him or risk losing my company. I just didn't know how to get out from under this debt. I couldn't just say, "You're not getting my company," because it was all documented in black and white. Plus, he had these big-gun lawyers.

The enormity of the situation was almost beyond my ability to grasp it. How could someone who had been so generous and helpful—someone who had been recommended by an esteemed local minister—have duped me like this? I had trusted him with my life's work and it almost didn't survive for me to tell the tale of it.

I remember when I hired the lawyer to help me fight for my business, and the look on his face when I explained my case. He looked at me as if he was thinking, "You're supposed to be this very astute businesswoman. Do you mean to tell me that you've signed a document and given your company away?" There was no use in explaining to him at this point how I had thought this was an upstanding businessman. I had thought that no one could say anything bad about this man. That I had essentially treated him as my business partner and friend, and that I thought he was going to do right by me. I had just learned the hard way that you can't trust on that level when it comes to business. Far stronger relationships than I had with this man have ended in betrayal by one partner or another.

I had no cause to trust on this level. It was a harsh lesson.

I would fight him for a year. It was a drain, too, because of all the legal bills I was wracking up. But in the end I prevailed. For legal reasons, I cannot divulge the details of how, but suffice it to say that I was able to legally regain 100 percent control of my company and I didn't have to pay back one thin dime of the money he "invested."

But there would be no resting on the laurels of this victory. It seems there was always another battle around the corner, and the next was quite near at hand.

SUCCESS INGREDIENT TWENTY-FIVE

Success does not make you immune to attack.

Chapter Twenty-Six

Growing Pains

In the end, freedom is a personal
and lonely battle.

—*Alice Walker, author*

I WAS VERY FORTUNATE that I was well into servicing Denny's during the fiasco where I nearly lost Michele Foods. The Denny's account enabled me to have consistent and adequate cash flow. But trouble was looming for me here, too. My relationship with Denny's was terrific, but problems cropped up in my relationship with my co-packer.

Let me explain exactly what a co-packer means to a business like mine. A co-packer is someone who owns a plant where your product can be made. Many companies like mine don't actually manufacture our own products. We pay someone else to make our formulated product and then we market and sell it afterward. It's hard to do everything.

It's kind of antiquated to say, "I'm going to go out here, and I'm going to pick the cotton. And then I'm going to go somewhere and I'm going to weave the cotton. And then I'm going to go somewhere and I'm going to make the garment. Then I'm going to find a store, and I'm going to go there and sell it." It's too complicated.

In my twenty years, I've had my share of challenges with various co-packers. In this case, the relationship was structured so that I was the company that serviced Denny's, while I hired the co-packer to actually make the product. It's called second-tier selling. This was the basic setup to which we agreed. I thought it was straightforward, simple, and clear. And for six years, this arrangement was fine.

Competitor and Partner

I began to see that the co-packer was, well, not very fond of the way the deal was structured. This company ordinarily produced confections and other such products, including syrups that they probably figured they could have sold to Denny's direct. So I was a competitor. When they signed on with me, though, we had an agreement that was written in no uncertain terms.

Eventually the co-packer grew weary of dealing with me as a middleman. He called Denny's one day and said, "We're no longer going to ship to Michele." Of course, this put Denny's on alert. Denny's had 17,000 restaurants. If the co-packer stopped shipping to me, Denny's would be out of syrup.

The co-packer did not understand the relationship that I had with Denny's. He did not care that Denny's specifically wanted to have relationships in place with diverse companies. He didn't care that the syrup he made for my company was just one part of the deal, that Denny's wanted the added value of working with a minority-owned and -operated company.

I'd had a great relationship with Denny's for six years. These were people that I liked, and I believed that they liked me. Just because I had co-packer problems, I was not going to cause problems for them.

I walked away and allowed them to go back and get a co-packer on their own. I thought it was important to take the high road, to maintain my relationship with Denny's— I have a different sort of deal with them today and an ongoing relationship—and to maintain the reputation of my firm. It had been a good six years; Denny's had been very good to me, and it gave me experience in the foodservice side of the business.

I can't divulge all the details of how this went, but the result was that my cash flow was severely hampered. It was no longer $300,000 a year in inflows. That had been money that I really relied on to grow Michele Foods. So this was another bang for me. I wondered how I could rebound. I didn't have room to have a bad month. I didn't have a lot of accounts back then. I only had Jewels, Dominick's, and Wal*Mart. And I wasn't moving a lot of product in those stores. The inflows from Denny's had been keeping me afloat.

The problems with the co-packer threatened to pull me under. But with prayer and with perseverance, and with a lot of faith and with good attorneys, they could not drown me. I managed to keep my head above water.

SUCCESS INGREDIENT TWENTY-SIX

It's always worth it to take the high road—but that doesn't mean it won't be costly.

Chapter Twenty-Seven

Turning It Around

People might not get all they work
for in this world, but they must
certainly work for all they get.

—*Frederick Douglass, abolitionist leader*

MEANWHILE, THERE WAS STILL other business to tend. I
had started a relationship with General Mills. I had
done a lot of research on General Mills, and I understood that
the company made this wonderful pancake mix, Bisquick, but
it didn't have a syrup product. I knew that it would be
stacked with value for them to do business with Michele
Foods. The company did not have much of a minority market
share. Its competitors that made pancakes also made syrup.

So I structured a deal and went and talked to the CEO of
General Mills and said, "This would be a great relationship
because you would get some African-American involvement;
you would get some minority market share, and I'm not a
competitor; I don't make pancakes. But I do make syrup. So
it gives me an opportunity to do business with you from a

retail standpoint. And all I ask you to do is to partner with me in the stores that we're both in. Let's cross-promote our products with a coupon."

General Mills knew a good thing when they saw it, so they agreed. And they agreed to pay for everything, which was great. We came up with a retail promotion where if you bought Michele's syrup and Bisquick you got $1 off.

Easing Off

I was also reaping the benefits of my relationship with Denny's, which had given me a lot of great publicity. The national spotlight eased my sales calls to other grocery chains. I found I was getting a lot better reception from buyers on whom I called. The relationship eventually helped me to attain placement of Michele's syrups in a number of other grocery chains, including Wal*Mart and some Kroger locations.

I went into such companies as Ahold USA, which was the parent company to Stop & Shop, and I met a wonderful gentleman—at the time the president of Stop & Shop—named Bill Grize, and Bill had started a diversity program. So I went into Stop & Shop. From there, I went into H-E-B in Texas. And wherever a diversity program or a diversity initiative was started, I was the first one at the door, or one of the first ones at the door, knocking on the door, exposing my product to them. And because I was in a position to ship anywhere and I understood how to transport product and how to incorporate it into my costs, I was able to branch out into such chains as BI-LO's, and the Safeways of the world, and expand my product line to include Maple Honey Crème and Butter Pecan syrups.

I had a good run with Denny's. I did not want to put them in a situation where I cried wolf and caused problems for them.

A Similar Fight

The experience with Denny's also prepared me for another incident where a company that I had brought an opportunity to tried to cut me out of the deal.

I met Hala Moddelmog, president of Church's Chicken, at a Women's Foodservice conference and told her that I thought Michele's Honey Crème Syrup would be a good application over their chicken and their shrimp. She advised me to call the diversity manager at America's Favorite Chicken, parent company of Church's Chicken, and talk to him about my interest in doing business with Church's. He put in place an opportunity for me to meet with Frank Belatti, who is president of America's Favorite Chicken (AFC).

I went to Atlanta and met with Mr. Belatti. He was a really likable, wonderful person who had a lot of grass-roots ideas and had come from a grass-roots background himself. I explained to him that Honey Créme went very well over their popcorn shrimp and their chicken and I'd like to sell it to AFC as a dip.

Frank thought about it, and then he said, "Michele, I don't think we do enough business for that. I don't think that would work." But on my way out the door, he stopped me and suggested that I talk to his colleague in procurement. That gentleman said, "Go match my condiments."

What that meant was he wanted me to go and take his condiments—the ketchup and the hot sauce and the jalapeño sauce and all of that—and match their formulation and give them a competitive price. Once again, because I don't own a plant, I had to find a co-packer. I found a company in Memphis, Tennessee, owned by a group of African-American guys. They had just purchased a plant Shoney's used to own. It was a plant that made condiments. I told them about AFC's desire to do business with me, and I presented them the opportunity for a joint venture with me to match the condiments in formula and give them a competitive price. I said that we could go in collectively to get this account. They agreed to come in with me, and I gave them the product specs and information that AFC had given to me. Nine months later, Church's came back to me and said, "Michele, it's almost time for us to renew the contract. We need to see your product line."

Unfortunately, we had not adequately matched the condiment formulas. So I left it alone. Disappointed, I explained our position to Mr. Belatti. Years later, however, I developed another joint venture with a large manufacturer and together we were able to successfully match their condiments. So I was back in the Church's family.

The end of my biggest contract with Denny's also helped me to realize that it was time for me to punch up my core strength: the syrup. I told Christale, "Now, what we have to learn how to do is to stand on our own and rely solely on what we started with—my products—Michele's Honey Crème, Butter Pecan, and Maple Crème syrups. Let's make sure that is producing to its fullest potential. That's our security. That's our legacy. That's our future."

SUCCESS INGREDIENT TWENTY-SEVEN

There's always something good to be gained out of a tough situation.

Chapter Twenty-Eight

Back to the Basics

There is nothing like returning to a
place that remains unchanged to
find the ways in which you yourself
have altered.

> —*Nelson Mandela, former president of*
> *South Africa, antiapartheid leader*

DURING THE FIRST TWENTY YEARS of my business, I was
dogged by co-packer problems, as I have already mentioned. By 2003, I was on my fourth one. Finding a co-packer
is not the easiest thing in the world to do. You have to find
one that you can really trust because you're literally turning
your product and your business over to someone. If that
someone is not honest or if something happens to his or her
business, then you could be out of business, too. So you have
to be careful. Plus, they're not just lying around for the
picking—you've got to find them.

So you can't simply jump from co-packer to co-packer.
When you pick one, it should be one that you can stick with

for as long as possible. Finding a new co-packer has also been challenging because my formulation is my own, and I have my own specs to it. So a co-packer has to deliberate to make certain that he can make my product. He has to do practice runs. The product has to be produced to my satisfaction.

The first co-packer I had was ready to jump ship and abandon me on my figuratively capsizing boat once he found out that, under the first formulation, the product was turning rancid on store shelves. He did not want to be associated with Michele Foods because he feared liability for his company. It was a mutual feeling. I didn't want him to be associated with my company because I believed that he could have alerted me to the problem with the formula sooner. So I got rid of that co-packer, and I reformulated my syrup. I found a second co-packer, and that co-packer ran afoul of me, too. This co-packer cut corners on my raw ingredients. They bought cheaper raw ingredients that made my product change colors. I was livid. Once again, I had to eat the cost of bad product and pull my product from shelves. And once again, I had to go find another co-packer.

I found the third co-packer, Kalva, in Gurnee, Illinois. My contact there knew the problems that I had previously, and he was able to correct them to my satisfaction. But, it wasn't meant to last. I packaged my product in glass and his plant was transitioning away from glass in favor of plastic. They didn't want to do glass because if glass breaks, the smallest little piece could float into a product and then you have a problem. Glass takes a more involved quality-control effort. A lot of plants do not like to pack in glass. But I insisted on glass because it was part of the uniqueness of my product.

So in between co-packer No. 3 phasing me out because I used glass, I transitioned into manufacturing my syrups myself. It was not something that I looked forward to at all! But I could not say, "Well for nine months I won't have a co-packer. Let me stop making product."

At the Vat

A decade had passed since I tried to sell syrup I made on the stove with my great-great-grandmother's original secret recipe, which spoiled the next day, and I had come a long way. Everything was different, but here I was making the syrup—and supervising other people making it—all over again.

It was 1993, the year that I was suffering from the brain tumor, although I did not know yet that I was that ill. So I was manufacturing syrup right along the same time that I had this tumor. This was, of course, pretty stressful. That's why everybody felt that I had a stress-related disease—because I had so much going on. They thought, once the stress is gone, you'll be okay.

Deciding to make the syrup myself without the assistance of a co-packer was, I feel, one of those shining moments where an entrepreneur has to rise to a challenge or go down in flames. I was in the middle of a booming business. I had picked up more accounts. So the last thing I needed to do was not to have a co-packer. I had never, ever missed delivering my product to retailers. I've never had to tell a retailer that I could not meet a purchase order. Whenever there was such a threat looming over my business, I always had the foresight to see it coming miles away. Each time there were problems on the horizon with a co-packer, I saw it coming and reacted accordingly.

As co-packer No. 3 was transitioning out of the job, I found help in a gentleman whose product, ironically, was egg rolls. At the time, this man was "mayor" of Chicago's China-town, and he had a plant there where he made these egg rolls. But he had the ability to warehouse product and he had vats. He had equipment so that I could literally make the product.

I talked to him about my problem, and he said, "You can use my plant, but I don't know how to make syrup." So I hired a chemist and I hired someone to oversee production. I brought Christale and my own staff of people in, and I literally made product for about nine months at this location. And it was a very different experience for me and my staff.

A Learning Experience

Overseeing production myself was my first real indication of what it costs to make my products. I had to buy all of the raw materials on my own, which was very eye-opening. That lesson was a tradeoff for the trouble of having to make the syrup on my own. On the other end, though, a good deal of money was tied up in inventory. Not so much finished goods inventory, but rather raw material inventory. If you buy a 100-pound tanker of corn syrup, that corn syrup may sit for a while.

I would go to the plant every morning around 6 P.M. and I would set up. I literally had to run this product every day because I could not yield as much in one run as when I had a co-packer, because we were hand-packing it.

We were making it in a big vat. Then we would actually go up on a stepladder to reach the vat. I would get this huge wooden spoon, and I would stir the product myself. It wasn't like stirring a pot on your kitchen stove! Once the product was stirred, we had to funnel it out of the big vat. Then we had to hand-pack it. We formed an assembly line. I had people standing on one side pouring, and I had people on the other side rinsing bottles and labeling the bottles. I had brought in my friends and my daughters' friends to work.

I would build up enough inventory so I did not have to scramble. If I had an order for 500 cases, I didn't wait until I got that order to make 500 cases. We would have inventory stacked up in a room, ready to fill my orders. Through all of this, we never missed delivering product. The product was always sitting on the shelves.

SUCCESS INGREDIENT TWENTY-EIGHT

You're never too important to stir the pot yourself—be willing to do what you have to do.

Chapter Twenty-Nine

From Scratch

The best way to predict your future
is to create it.

—*Patti LaBelle, singer*

IMPORTANT LESSONS OFTEN COME OUT OF STRIFE. Doing all the procurement in 1997 was a real eye-opener for me. I didn't know a thing about it at that time, and it wasn't as though Christale had a class on the subject in college. We learned together, the only way we could—we picked up the phone and got started. We'd call suppliers and say, "We want to order enough corn syrup to make 800 cases of product." And then someone on the other end of the phone had to say, "Well, this is what we have for you to choose from. Some comes packaged in a 100-pound weight, and some of them come in a 1-pound weight. Some of them come in ounces."

Behind the closed doors, we had to learn things that huge companies staffed by M.B.A.s already know. No one was going to tell me, "Okay, Michele. This is how you buy raw materials." That's not how it works.

If someone is making my product for me and charging me $15 a case when it costs $8 a case for them to make, why would that someone tell me, "Okay, Michele, you know for years and years I've been charging this price because I can. You've allowed me to procure all of your raw materials and this is what it's costing you. By the way, here's what we've paid for your raw materials, and this is where it all comes from."

At the end of the day, if you want the information that will allow you to save money, you've got to figure it out yourself.

Down to It

I had to go back to the formulation for the syrup. I thought about what goes into the product. Because I knew what goes into the product, I was able to start figuring out how I could make it without a co-packer. When I went into that manufacturing mode, I had no choice but to figure it out. I had to source out my own honey, my own butter buds, my own corn syrup, my own flavor ingredients, my own bottles—everything. I learned to strive to get the lowest cost from the very bottom of the manufacturing process for better margins on the other end. Once I learned how to do my own procurement, I just got really addicted to it and I wouldn't let anybody buy my raw materials.

The next co-packer made the product with the raw materials I provided, and from 1997 until 2001, Christale did all the procurement of raw materials for Michele Foods. It was a whole different process, but it helped me in growing a company. How can you grow a company and not know what your paper clips costs, or what your paper costs or your ink costs or your employees cost? The same thing is true in food. How am I growing a company if I don't understand what honey—a main ingredient—costs?

There are two types of charges with a co-packer—a toll charge and a service charge. After I learned to do my own procurement, I paid only a toll charge, which is the cost for actual labor and other overhead related to making your product. If the co-packer charges you $2 a case, then within that $2, you're paying for hourly labor. You're paying for the co-packer's lights to be on. You're paying for their equipment. You're paying for all of that within that $2. The toll charge is all I should have been paying, I learned. Instead, I was also paying a service charge. If you know your costs of raw materials and you get them yourself, then you can save a heap of money because you can avoid the service charge. The service charge is assessed when the co-packer buys your raw materials and brings them into the plant to make your product. In doing that I was able to reformulate the product, so I bought the best ingredients—ingredients that were cost-effective enough for me to get my case costs down so that I could start making money.

Oh, Honey!

After nearly a year of searching, I found Honey Tree, a co-packer in Onsted, Michigan. Honey Tree is the company that

I drove to with my map and a magnifying glass when my tumor was affecting my eyesight. It's a good thing they turned out to be a worthy company.

This is how I found Honey Tree. I had always bought honey from a honey seller called John Straub, who was preparing to sell his business. So he was in transition. But he didn't yet have a buyer. He needed a connection. So I stopped and tried to help him find that connection, and I found Honey Tree. I helped him to find a buyer, and in turn I got another co-packer. The new buyers were in a position to make my syrup. So his problem got solved, and so did mine. So my good deed bounced back on me.

I believe that you have to always be willing to stretch. And in stretching, you have to always look at who's around you and if they're stretching, too. Then you need to say, "Okay, let me help you stretch." And in stretching and helping someone else to stretch, you end up getting double the value.

Making the Margins

In the food business, you're working on margins. Anytime you put a penny or two or three onto your costs, it drives down your margins. Everyone tries to work within certain margins. There are certain margins that I need to make in order to be on a certain path and to be successful. There are certain margins that the co-packer makes. And the retailer has to sell to the consumer in order to make a certain margin.

So the lower your costs are, the better margins you can get. All of the co-packers prior to Honey Tree charged me by the case—making use of the fact that I didn't know what my ingredients cost. I would never be that way again.

With better margins, you can better package your product. You can better transport your product. You can discount your product and have sales promotions. You can advertise your product.

SUCCESS INGREDIENT TWENTY-NINE

A tough situation can be an opportunity for valuable learning.

Chapter Thirty

What Entrepreneurs Are Made Of

Talent is like electricity. We don't
understand electricity. We use it.
—*Maya Angelou, writer*

ENTREPRENEURS ARE VERY STRANGE PEOPLE. But I think that if you get a good one, with a good idea and with the three elements, the three Ps—patience, passion, and perseverance—the outcome of that is going to be something that's going to help society by adding something new to medicine or to the retail chains or even to the arts.

Entrepreneurs aren't just people who own businesses. All the Puffy Combs and the Halle Berrys of the world are entrepreneurs in their own right. They're performers and actors, but they're working on ways to run their own lives. They use their talent to become entrepreneurs. Like J. Lo and her perfumes, Russell Simmons and his clothing. And Oprah is doing a multitude of entrepreneurial things. Everything she touches is entrepreneurial to a degree.

The Creative Mind

Entrepreneurs are individuals who you really don't want to try to harness. Sooner or later, you will have to release them. People don't understand them because they're creative. The world isn't always welcoming of creativity. Because entrepreneurs don't always get from others the nurturing that they require, they have to nurture themselves. They have to chisel their way to what's inside of them.

One thing about entrepreneurs that is important to know: We don't give up. It's just not part of the code. You encounter a problem, and it's grist for the mill, par for the course, or whatever you want to call it. You handle it and keep moving forward. If your boat capsizes near an island, you don't just say, "Well, the boat capsized. I'm marooned. So let me just live here on this island." No! You have a mission. You're trying to get back on home ground. So you need to either figure out how to fix the boat or build yourself a new boat. That's the entrepreneur's spirit. And it's the entrepreneur's spirit that built America. It's the entrepreneur's spirit that continues to build companies from the ground up. This is the spirit in which I always deal with my problems, big or small. Sometimes the big ones have seemed as if they could doom my operation. But it depends on your perspective.

The School of Hard Knocks

People have a tendency to assume that if a child goes through four years of college, and then goes back for a master's or a doctorate, that kid can run the world some day. But it's not always that simple. What about the child's personality and natural talents? You can't leave that out. Someone might have the education, but not the personality to do a particular thing.

That's why a lot of times people have all of this education and they can't find a job. It takes more than an academic education to survive out here. On the other hand, sometimes the uneducated person has all the other tools needed to succeed in life, and all they need is the education. They don't always go to a brick-and-mortar institution to get educated. Sometimes they go to the school of hard knocks, where there's open admission. At the school of hard knocks, it doesn't matter who you are or what you have or don't have. You've just got to be ready to work it as long and as hard as you must.

It didn't take a master's or a doctorate degree for Oprah to become a billionaire. It took a certain type of personality. You don't hear much about her education credentials. Of course, she went to school. She's very educated. But that's not why she's a billionaire. She's a billionaire for all of the other reasons that it takes in order to be successful: perseverance, passion, faith, belief in herself—all the strong qualities that she has. We don't know what education Donald Trump has either. I mean, has anyone ever told you how many degrees he has? Probably not! But you know that he is rich and powerful.

Some of the greatest entrepreneurs in the world never went to school at all. Education does not denote dollars. There are some poor geniuses out there.

A lot of times people put so much emphasis on formal education, but the real knowledge comes and sticks to you when you get knocked down, get up, and get knocked down again.

As an entrepreneur, you do not get paid based on your education. In corporate America, you might be able to go right into a certain salaried position—$50,000 for this degree; $70,000 for that this one, or $100,000 for that one. But once you're tied into that, you can only make that. That's why they call it a salary cap, because the work you do for someone else has its limits. You could be the smartest individual in the world, but if you're only limited to what that salary or that dollar rate is, how can you become anything more? You've got to step out of that! That's just the way it is. In order not to have a ceiling on your money-earning potential, you have to be outside the box. And most people outside the box have to be entrepreneurs. You have to be someone who invents something, who perfects something, who brings something different, who meets a need, or who creates a need. You have to take your own little dream and make it into reality.

I'm not anti-education. I'm far from it. I just believe that too many students are unprepared for real-world challenges because they lean too much on the formalized learning process. I would take the school of hard knocks degree over a master's or a doctorate any day. At the school of hard knocks, even when it appears you've earned an F, the cumulative effects can surpass any A-plus mark you could ever earn by sitting in someone's classroom and checking little boxes with the "right" answers.

The Road Less Traveled

When you start off on your road to being an entrepreneur, no one's going to stop and say, "Oh, wait a minute. Let me give you a course on entrepreneurship." Entrepreneurship is filled with moments of discovery and serendipity—the lessons that you earn through your trials. If you come at entrepreneurship from corporate America, you might be thrown. There's a big difference between the way entrepreneurs approach things and the way someone from a corporation might approach the same problem. For the person coming from corporate structure, things may have been a breeze. You've been traveling along this highway that has already been built. You're sharing it with others who were zooming up and down this convenient infrastructure. There are railings. There's a shoulder on the main thoroughfare. And, look, there's a toll booth.

When you're an entrepreneur, however, you often have to take the dirt road that's way off the beaten path to get to where you're going. You don't have concrete paving. There's no one at a toll booth raising money to pay for improvements or to give you directions. This road might not even be on anybody's radar. But this is the direction that you've chosen. So it's a little harder to get by. If you come out of a corporate environment, you have to get out of the corporate mindset. In a corporation, lots of stuff is predone for you. When you go in, someone may tell you, "Okay, this is what our costs are. These are our suppliers with the most competitive pricing." Your job, in fact, might have a sort of template. You're probably not the first to do it at XYZ Corporation. It's structured and it's been done over and over again. Many of the people working with you are just like you. They came to their positions after moving up the ladder. They started rungs below just after finishing college or getting an M.B.A. When you are an entrepreneur, a lot of what you learn in school and in corporate America will apply, but a lot of it won't. It's a different world. It's a world of people who have belief that they can do anything. They believe that if the mind can conceive it, it can manifest.

SUCCESS INGREDIENT THIRTY

If you believe you can do anything, you can—and you will.

Chapter Thirty-One

Media Might

You'll find that when you're free,
your true creativity, your true self
comes out.

—Tina Turner, singer/songwriter

MOST HUGE CORPORATIONS HAVE HUGE BUDGETS that they leverage in all possible mediums to bring attention to their products. They carefully craft campaigns. They spend lots of money for the perfect logo and the perfect slogan. They dream of coming up with the next catch phrase. They woo big-name celebrities and pay them the big bucks to drink a soft drink or wear a pair of sneakers or underwear. They animate cartoon people or animals.

For smaller companies with similar products this can be intimidating. It's like, how do you even begin to contend with that kind of might?

I've been asking this of myself for nearly twenty years. In the syrup category, everybody knows the big brand syrups out there. Everybody's heard of Hungry Jack; everybody's heard of Aunt Jemima; and everybody's heard of Mrs. Butter-worth's. But not everybody's heard of Michele's, because I haven't been able to tell everybody. I don't have the dollars to tell everybody.

David to Goliath

When I get product into a store in Lakeland, Florida, for example, nobody knows that I'm there. Who there have I told? I haven't told the consumer by television. I haven't told the consumer by radio. I haven't told the consumer by news-paper. I haven't told the consumer by knocking on his door. But the product next to mine is on television and radio and in print. So when I enter a new market, it's tough to move even one case per store because no one knows I'm there. The only person I've told is the chain's buyer, the person who said, "Okay, we'll put you on our shelves, but once you're there, you need to perform." Talk about pressure! I don't have to pay slotting fees, and I'm taking shelf space from another item that might have been selling thousands of bottles a week. So I have to look as good and as strong on the shelf as the major brands.

So I have to say, "Okay, if they're running promotions, what can I do? I can't do TV commercials with a little bottle of syrup walking across the screen. I don't have the funds that they have, so I have to do something that involves little to no money. So I have to be very creative in a manner that is far-reaching." This is the task I am faced with daily.

It's been very challenging to be able to stay on these shelves for twenty years without readily available advertising and marketing dollars. How have I made it work? It just has! I believe it's because I set out for the journey and I declared, success or bust, and I won't settle for bust. As I've always maintained, the tools that you need will appear eventually. You've just got to be committed to working around not having them until they show up.

The Gifts of Presence

I've often been asked how much mileage I get out of being featured in magazines and on TV news shows and being interviewed about my company. Media attention has helped Michele Foods on a number of levels. I was mainly selling in the Chicago market for nine years. And I always made sure that I was on the scene. I had a presence at every event that I could to raise awareness. Eventually, I got pretty decent play in the local media. In fact, it was presence in the local media—a TV news segment—that helped me to land my product in Wal*Mart and thus widen my distribution beyond the Midwest.

After I got the Denny's account, they included me in a media blitz and I ended up in some very prestigious national publications, from daily newspapers to magazines, including *Fortune* and the *Wall Street Journal*. I also was blessed to get some national TV coverage. Unfortunately, I wasn't always in a position to take advantage of the coverage I've gotten nationally. It could be frustrating to be blessed with such a far reach, but only be able to reap the benefits on a limited basis. I knew that if I got local media coverage in Chicago, I would move product out of Jewel and Dominick's. But if a national article was written and you read about me in Texas, for instance, you couldn't buy the syrup because I didn't have distribution in Texas.

So the PR helped, but at times it wasn't the biggest factor. I've come to realize that PR is the type of thing where if you read about something, you don't run out to the store and buy it right then and there. For instance, I've been hearing about this incredible self-help book in the media and I said, "I'm going to go to the bookstore and buy that one." But even after Christale came into the office reading her own copy one day and I said again that I would get it, I still haven't gotten the darned thing. So if someone reads about Michele's syrups, and says, "Oh, great! That sounds really good," they don't always put on their clothes and run to the store, and I don't necessarily see a surge in sales.

I realize that everything I've ever done—from telling someone on the street about my syrups to doing festivals in a park to accommodating media interviews—has helped me to sell a bottle of syrup. Through a variety of channels that may cost you little in money, you may make a connection with a customer. A person hears about you or meets you in person at a festival or someone else mentions your product fondly, and then maybe you begin to take up space in that person's consciousness.

People are often on autopilot with brands they've grown to know and trust and love. Sometimes it takes a lot for them to stray. It takes more than just one article or television segment or festival appearance. What I'm saying is that every effort melds together and if it's the right combination, you may end up with exceptional results. With every layer, your product becomes part of the collective thought. You may become more than a human interest story. Maybe you become a regular item on someone's grocery list, but it can take awhile. The sooner you're able to grow into massive media attention, the sooner you can reap the benefits.

Human Interest More Than Syrup Interest

Of course, the benefits can be hard to quantify. You see a sweater in the sales papers that you want and there's a coupon for a percentage off the purchase. You put the coupon in your purse, and you forget about it until the sale is over. People don't always move on things. Everything is so gradual.

So when you're small, you can't expect that wider exposure will be the savior for your company. But you'd do well to appreciate it and figure out how to get the most mileage you can from it.

Early on, I noticed something about the media. They weren't all that interested in the syrup, per se. No reporter that I can recall has ever really written a story about the syrup. They don't go on and on with questions about how fabulously unique the syrup is or want to discuss my brand character statement or anything of the sort. They've always focused on one of three things: my great-great-grandmother's peculiar legacy of handing the syrup down through the third daughter in each generation, my struggle to bring the syrup to market, and my experiences as an African-American woman running a small business.

Of course, during the first few interviews or so, I wanted to talk about how great the syrup is and why it should be chosen over my competitors. To me, it was about the syrup. To them, it was about a story—a human interest story. Even though I may have ended up in the business section, the focus always came back to the human interest aspect. Here I was bent on pushing the syrup out on its merits, the fact that it's really a great product. But reporters always wanted to focus on America Washington.

I'm proud of the legacy, of course. I guess it had been around in my family for so long that I didn't see it right away as a human interest story. Through the eyes of others, I started to see that the tradition is pretty interesting. Then the more I thought about it, the more I could appreciate how deep it is. A slave started a tradition that set me free in the 1980s.

SUCCESS INGREDIENT THIRTY-ONE

Your own creativity can make up a lot for money you don't have.

Chapter Thirty-Two

Dealing with Diversity

I truly believe that individuals can
make a difference in society. Since
periods of change such as the
present one come so rarely in
human history, it is up to each of us
to make the best use of our time to
help create a happier world.

—*The Dalai Lama of Tibet*

THE MEDIA HAS ALWAYS BEEN INTERESTED in *my* human
interest story, too. The story of America Washington's act
of sending the recipe through the ages went well with the
story of how I turned the legacy into a somewhat unusual
business. You have to go back twenty years with me on this
one. When I was just starting this business, people thought it
a peculiar thing because black people were doing a lot of other
things, but they were not entrepreneurs in the food industry.

This was not a business that we went to school to learn
about or that we grew up in. We weren't getting degrees in

food management. We were consumers in this business. We weren't manufacturers and distributors. We hardly even had jobs at the retail level as far as I could see. We may have had jobs bagging groceries, or working as cashiers or stock boys. But that was about it. We had mom-and-pop stores in our communities, but how many African-American-owned grocery store chains do we own even today? It's an industry that has been a good-old-boy system for years and years and years.

We were locked out of it. It was like white America was saying to black America, "Okay, we control the food supply. We control how it gets to you and we'll tell you how much it costs to eat." It was an industry that hired minorities for the menial part of it, one where white men held the upper echelon jobs. To me, *these* were the peculiar things.

With these conditions, my entrance into this industry stood out, and that's another reason I got attention. It could have been just about any food product in my hand and I would have been noticed.

A Common Language

I was always in situations in which I had to walk into an environment and talk to people whose language I didn't know, and I'm not talking about English! But, no matter that, I still had to persuade them coming in the door that they needed to put my product on their shelves. It was like a culture change for me. I wasn't raised to interact with white males. What African-American woman has been? I didn't go to school with them. I had never learned to negotiate with them.

I was out here for eleven years before I went into an office and saw a black woman as a buyer in the breakfast category. She worked for Kroger. I've seen more since then, but it took a while.

In the last eleven or twelve years, I've seen more black diversity officials. Some corporations still have white women and white men in charge of their diversity programs. Now you go figure that one. That still confuses me. How can a white woman or a white male fully understand what it's like—and what it takes—to really achieve diversity?

So it's still a situation where if we don't get into this business and learn this business and pass this business on, we'll still be locked out of it. And it's one of the largest money-makers around. Food. Everybody has to eat. Everybody has to go to the grocery store at some time.

Part of Making a Better Environment

I've become a bit of a diversity officer myself. I don't hesitate to ask a company that I'm working with how many minority- and women-owned businesses they do business with, and I've been recognized in a number of ways for these kinds of efforts.

For example, in 2000, I received the Phenomenal Women Award at the V-103's Expo for Today's Black Woman in Chicago and among the recipients were Juanita Jordan, Linda Johnson-Rice, and *Chicago Sun-Times* columnist Mary

Mitchell. It was an incredible experience; we were all seated at the same table. It was unforgettable to be one among these women.

The Phenomenal Women Award is bestowed annually by WVAZ-FM and Merry Green Promotional Group, which was founded by Merry Green, who has become a close friend.

SUCCESS INGREDIENT THIRTY-TWO

Staying connected to your community is a source of strength.

Chapter Thirty-Three

The Queen of Them All

The way to choose happiness is to
follow what is right and real and the
truth for you. Live your own. And
you will for sure know the meaning
of happiness.

—Oprah Winfrey, talk show pioneer, actress,
producer/creator, magazine founder and
editorial director, educator, philanthropist

OF COURSE, THERE ARE SOME MEDIA EXPERIENCES that give
me more than a little publicity, and there are some
African-Americans who have achieved the extraordinary.

Doing *The Oprah Winfrey Show* is the queen of them all.
The first time I did her show was in 1999. I had gotten the
Denny's contract and Michele Foods had made several mil-
lion dollars. Oprah had the millionaire minute show, and we
were invited to participate. I had gotten to the point by then
where I felt really confident that I understood the business.
I had growing distribution and understood distribution.

I was getting regular publicity, which was really helping to push the product through to consumers. People knew about the product.

We were growing and we were making money. And then, Oprah called and asked me to do her show. Immediately, I remembered that day about fifteen years earlier when I had met her at the makeup counter in Marshall Field's department store. She had commented that we would cross paths again, and here would be the golden moment.

A Great Boost

It would be unlike any press experience I'd ever had. After we did her show, the effect was the most immediate. Wherever we were in distribution, we sold product. If we were in ninety Wal*Marts, we saw a surge in ninety Wal*Marts. We still weren't saturated all over the country, but we were able to maximize to the hilt wherever we were. It was a great boost.

A year after my first appearance, I heard from Oprah again. A viewer who had seen my first appearance had contacted her about it, because my message of creating your own destiny had reached her at a critical time in her life and turned her around.

This appearance led viewers to the stores again. When I told her on the show how much she'd helped my business, it's because she really did. Had I not been on her show, I don't think I would have grown as fast as I have grown in these past few years.

The Real Deal

People always ask what it's like to make an appearance on the show, so I'll tell you.

When we were asked to do Oprah's show, we went into Oprah "camp." And what Oprah camp meant to us is that everything stops and our focus shifts to preparing to do the show. There's nothing more important than doing a good Oprah show! So much is going to come out of it. There are so many positives in it. I mean, you're walking into the world of a woman who has done what everyone in the world would love to do: She's made herself a billionaire. From the time that they ask you to be a guest to the time that the limousine picks you up from your home, you're riding in this limousine as Oprah's guest. You pull up in front of Oprah's studio and you get out of this limousine, and the doors open for you. Someone greets you pleasantly, "Are you Michele? Let me direct you to the Green Room." You go into the Green Room, and you sit there and you have hors d'oeuvres. You have fruit. You have Coke. You have all of the little nice things to eat. And they do your makeup. They do your hair. They prepare you for Oprah. I felt really blessed.

Oprah's studio is really intimate. There are only about 300 to 350 people in the audience. You're among a select group if you're in front of the camera. The first time we did her show, it was live, but it didn't feel live. You may be in front of millions of millions of people, but you don't see them. You see the camera and the camera operators, but you eventually tune them out. Once you start talking to Oprah, it's like talking to a girlfriend. It's just you and her and the subject you're talking about. It doesn't register that this camera's going to all of these millions and millions of people.

It's not as intimidating as it is when you're standing somewhere live on a stage trying to talk to a lot of people, because you are looking in people's faces and you see how many throngs of them there are out there. Then you may start to wonder if you're saying something and they're going, "Ooh!" and they're happy about it, or if they're going, "Ugh!" On *Oprah,* you don't get that kind of feedback from the audience, and that's why it's not as intimidating as if you were in front of even ten people live that could judge you with their reaction.

When Oprah finally walks out she brings you up on the stage and she addresses you and talks to you directly, and you see yourself in her eyes. You see the years of hard work and sacrifice reflected back from her. And at the same time, you see a girlfriend, a completely personable person. Your being there feels as if she appreciates what it took. The three times I've been a guest, I have thanked her personally while on the air. I've thanked her because, first of all, she's a role model for every African-American woman. She's a role model for women, period. She's a role model for entrepreneurs. She's a role model for businesspeople. She's a role model for spirituality. She's a role model on so many levels. And you are honored enough to be in her presence. That's how I felt. I was especially ecstatic because she requested my participation. She requested me. It puts you in a different place, I tell you.

She has such an overwhelmingly positive aura. There's intensity just in holding her hand. You're caught up in that energy, too. When you walk into Oprah's studio, you're caught up in this vortex; you're in awe of her. It's like Oprah's world. I always think, "Here's a woman who has written her own destiny." And she keeps daily company with other extraordinary individuals who have written their own destinies. On every wall in every hallway and in every room, all you see are images of extraordinary people. She's taken pictures with Bill Cosby, Nelson Mandela, President Clinton, Maria Shriver, and many others. You just see her face with everybody. It's really awesome to be in her studio, and the thrill goes on.

The Lesson of True Gratitude

They say that whenever you really want anything in life, you're supposed to request it at your happiest. I know that everyone has had the day where they just brought their car in from an accident. It's raining outside. The car's going to cost $500 to fix. You've got a headache and walk into the house and trip and bust your lip when you fall. Everybody's had those kinds of days. Those are the days when you may find it hard to say, "Well, let me just stop and be happy," and "Let me just stop and believe that I'm going to win a million dollars tomorrow."

But if you really want something, you can't draw it to you in an unhappy state. You can't get it saying, "Oh, I really hate my life. Why doesn't anything good ever happen for me?" When you're happy, you're in tune with the universal law of positiveness and all of the things that manifest to make a great day or a wonderful moment. You get up one day, and it's just a good day. It's 80 degrees outside; the sun is shining. You've got a brand-new car. You're in love. You're going on a trip. You just won the lottery or just got a bonus—all of those things lift you up off of your feet and make you feel good. Everyone has had those days.

The times that I have been asked to be on *Oprah* have been some of the happiest of my years in business—of my life, really. Those are times that lifted me and made me feel that I could do anything—at the very least get into a new grocery chain. I continue to draw from that happiness and from that positiveness. I have sat in her company and she has expressed interest in my accomplishments. It made me walk away and think, "You know what? I can do anything. I can go back to the office, and I can do some stuff now." She makes you feel good about who you are. She has elevated her life to a point where when she pats you on the back, you feel especially qualified.

SUCCESS INGREDIENT THIRTY-THREE

A good role model will elevate you: She has a magical effect.

Chapter Thirty-Four

The Challenges of Partnership

You don't need a certain number of
friends, only a number of friends
you can be certain of.
　　　　　　　—*Patti LaBelle, singer*

A FTER MY RUN WITH HONEY TREE, I went back into manufacturing for a second time in 2000. Honey Tree was a
small plant up in Michigan, and I was in Wal*Mart and my
volume was picking up beyond their capacity to fill orders.
I needed a co-packer who would not be overwhelmed when I
got to 800 and 900 cases; a co-packer that could automatically
have another run scheduled when I was selling that amount of
product. They could not meet the volume. So another co-
packer bit the dust, and I set out to find someone else.

My search for another co-packer lead me to start
thinking about manufacturing, because I found out about a
plant that made syrup that was up for sale in Cleveland. The

guy that owned it had gotten old. It had been in his family for a long time. In fact, it's a cute story associated with this plant. It was a plant that made syrup and when Ray Kroc first started McDonald's, the plant owner's father was in charge of the business. He was asked to make McDonald's orange syrup for their orange drink. But the owner said that he didn't see any future in a twenty-five-cent hamburger, and he declined the business! So instead they built their business making syrup and syrup toppings.

And so I looked into purchasing it. I was very serious about it. I brought some people to the table to see if they could help me determine how feasible it would be to do this, because co-packers had been such a problem for my business.

All the while, I continued my search for a co-packer, just in case. I found a plant in Broadview, Illinois. They started making the product for me, with Michele Foods handling procurement of raw materials. I looked briefly into buying that plant, too. Ultimately, though, I saw that I was not in a position to make such a move. I realized that I still did not have the manufacturing experience that it takes to run a plant.

So I switched focus from buying a plant to partnering with an existing plant to some degree. I wanted a different model in which a plant could make the product for me, and handle the procurement of raw materials in a mutually beneficial arrangement. That's the arrangement I set up with the next co-packer, the one that I am with right now.

Consultants and Such

Partnering is always complicated. One of the first things that you learn when you embark on an entrepreneurial journey is that you can't really depend on anyone but yourself. No matter how much you lean on someone else, at the end of the day, if it's your dream that you've put into play, you bear the ultimate responsibility for it. That makes you very protective of your creation. Of course, you look outside of yourself sometimes for information or advice. It can be helpful, but it can also be very frustrating.

Take using consultants, for example. I've said this time and time again: Consultants have been one of my worst nightmares.

You have to learn through experience and hard knocks how to gauge the right people for your organization. You're moving fast. You're at a point where you believe that you need a consultant. I used to have consultants come in and I would sign the first contract. And it would be devastating to me. Someone comes to your door, and you meet with him. You say, "Okay, I like you." But it might not be for the best reasons. It's not unlike finding the right mate. When you're dating, you might meet someone and think, "I like the way your shoes look. I like the way you look. Maybe you're the right one." Then after you get to know the person better you say, "You know what? Forget how the shoes look. Forget how he's dressed. Forget how he talked or how he looked. Is he bringing what I need to the table?"

Independent consultants usually come out of corporate America or they've left some field that they were in to become an entrepreneur. They often carry the knowledge and structure of their corporate upbringing with them and they're also trying to put their own spin on it. Then they meet you and they feel like you're this little entrepreneur and they have more knowledge than you have about what you're doing. They want to tell you how to do it better—which means their way, of course. And that's the worst thing you could do to an entrepreneur—tell them how to run their stuff your way. Sometimes people come with an agenda that I'm not ready for. Sometimes people come with an agenda that I have already done. So then you have a conflict. You'll listen for a while until they come up against something that in your gut you feel is not right for you. Then, you have to do one of two things. Let them down easy or just fire 'em! Either way, they usually have to go.

It's very difficult when you're an entrepreneur to listen to a lot of people, because this is your dream. And how can someone step into your dream and tell you how to dream? That's like someone waking you up in the middle of the night and saying, "Wait a minute. What are you dreaming?" And you say, "Uh, I was dreaming about . . ." Then they say, "Well, look, stop dreaming about that, and dream about this because this is what I think you should dream about." I have had this experience with a lot of individuals—consultants and other people who have come into my business and wanted to be a partner. They want to force their own ideas on me, but this is my dream. Let me dream my dream.

It's very hard to give an entrepreneur advice. What advice are you giving them? From whose dream are you taking this advice? Whose experiences? You might have done another product, but it didn't come from where mine came from. You weren't the same person doing it. You didn't have the same life experiences I've had. You may have had them generally, but not specifically.

A consultant that comes in has never been a single mom on welfare trying to do this. Had a brain tumor while doing this. Been on the verge of homelessness while doing this. So where is his or her experience coming from? Not from staying up all night and working by candlelight because the rent was due in two days, and couldn't be paid without selling four or eight or twelve cases of syrup.

For me, it's been ups and downs, and downs and ups. So no one can come in and say, "You know what, I've had that same life experience. This is what I did, and you should do the same." I never buy into that approach.

SUCCESS INGREDIENT THIRTY-FOUR

Trust yourself and your own experience. Be your own best support.

Chapter Thirty-Five

Daughters of the Trust

Most mothers are instinctive
philosophers.

—Harriet Beecher Stowe,
author of Uncle Tom's Cabin

MICHELE FOODS IS A UNIQUE KIND of family-run business.
First of all, a man didn't start it. Nor did a couple—a
mom and pop—start it. It's not run by a bunch of aunts and
uncles, cousins, and other various family members. Michele
Foods is a woman with two of her three daughters.

My daughters are my world. We're really close; we all
talk every day. We shop together. We go to dinner together.
We laugh together. We all have a great sense of humor.

You know, I never had sisters. I never had a lot of cousins.
I never had a lot of friends. So I was fortunate enough to be
able to birth friends, to have three girls who are my friends.
They are my best friends. Truly. When I need them as friends,
they're there as friends. When they need me as a mother, I
become the mother. We have a really flexible relationship.

Sibling Rivalry

So it's interesting, because these are daughters, these are young women, and these are individuals.

I have special relationships with my girls. I have three different daughters, so I have three different perspectives. And all three of these daughters are different. And they all kind of vie for my time and my love in their own way. I try to not do for one what I can't do for the others, but it's never equal.

So I'm Mama to Rosalyn. I'm Mama to Christale. I'm Mama to Keisha. But I'm a Mama to all of them in different ways. You know, I'm not Rosalyn's mother and boss. But I am Christale's mother and boss. I'm not Christale's mother and boss and homekeeper. But Keisha is under my roof, which can be difficult for both of us. I'm her mother. I'm her boss, and then I'm also her landlord and her roommate to some degree. So I'm here at the house talking about, "Take out the garbage." While I'm at work I'm talking about, "Fax this piece of paper." And I'm her mama talking about, "No, I don't think you should do that."

And when she's at home with me, she's like my room-mate. If I leave the bath water running, she won't say, "Mommy, I'm going to turn off your water." She'll say, "Michele! Girl, turn off your water." So it can be a lot of fun. It's certainly always interesting, but it also can be really trying at times.

I think, though, that through it all, we have emerged as a strong unit. We have risen to the promises of the legacy.

I think that America Washington would be ecstatic if she could see what her creation brought about in us.

It has meant so much to me to be able to show my daughters a different way of life. I have tried to show them that they have choices. They have choices because I've made sure that I had choices and that they had choices as well. You can work with me on my dream and take ownership in it, too. But it's okay if you want to work someplace other than Michele Foods.

Rosalyn chose a different path. She is a deputy sheriff with the Cook County Sheriff's Office, and I am very proud of her.

My Support in the Early Years

Although she has never worked full-time with Michele Foods, Rosalyn contributed much to the foundations of the company. As my oldest, she took on a lot of responsibility for running the household and caring for her sisters while I worked at establishing Michele Foods. She was the one who baby-sat. I could walk out of the house and go do something because I knew that she was in charge. She was always the really responsible one. So I depended on her in times when I had to work odd hours or work on weekends or leave town to do a trade show or simply sit in the office trying to figure out this business. She learned how to cook early on so she could feed her sisters. She did Keisha's hair. She would do the laundry. She took Keisha to school and picked her up.

Even when I was going through the divorce, Rosalyn was the one who I could depend on from the responsibility standpoint. She was really my support. If I could imagine a really supportive spouse, he would be like Rosalyn was. She really made sure that I had flexibility. And even when I needed to entertain myself, to go roller-skating or to do some of the things that I needed to do to break the monotony of trying to run this company, she always made sure I could have a break.

My success lagged way behind her maturing into a young woman. She was already well into her late teens by the time I started this business. She was going through her prom and then graduating from high school. So she wanted to start making her own way in the world as soon as she could. She wanted to have her own apartment. She wanted to have her own car.

She wanted to do things that, if she had stuck with me, she probably wouldn't have had at that time in her life. She decided against putting her life on hold to follow my dream, and I respect that. Her life went in the direction that she wanted it to go. We were still living in low-income housing by the time Rosalyn had turned twenty-one. She was like, "I'm ready to get out of here. I'm ready to grow up and live in a place of my own choice and means."

Rosalyn had to go through a lot of training to win her job as a sheriff's deputy. Once she got it, she embraced it and she became very career driven in that. She has been in that job ever since. She wasn't the type of person to jump from job to job. She picked a career and she stuck with it.

But, to this day, whenever I need her, Rosalyn's there in any way she can be to support Michele Foods. She'll take off a day from work here and there if I really need help at a trade show or whenever we've wanted to rally around the business in media interviews or on TV shows. In anything we do to promote Michele Foods from a family perspective, she's always been a part of that.

It's a very comforting feeling to know that I can pick up the phone and call Rosalyn at any time, and if I need something, she gets right over here. She also is the mother of my first and only grandchild thus far, Lindsey. And they are both very special to me.

I'm pretty sure that at some point in time, Rosalyn would love to come and be a part of the family business. At some point in the future, I would love to have her here, if she so chooses.

SUCCESS INGREDIENT THIRTY-FIVE

Give thanks for the precious support that you have.

Chapter Thirty-Six

Mom the Boss

When you make loving others the story of
your life, there's never a final chapter,
because the legacy continues. You lend your
light to one person, and he or she shines it on
another and another and another.

> —*Oprah Winfrey, talk show pioneer, actress,*
> *producer/creator, magazine founder and*
> *editorial director, educator, philanthropist*

VERY SELDOM DO AFRICAN-AMERICAN young women get a chance to be a part of a family business. My business has always been open to all of my daughters, but the two who have made the choice to join me are Christale and Keisha. Christale has been with me eleven years, and Keisha's been with me two years.

Basement Beginnings

Keisha started from the basement. She was just sitting there at nine years old, not knowing what she was doing. Because she was the youngest, with less homework than her sisters and more need to be close by me, she was recruited to do this. She didn't have much of a choice back then. As she grew up, she had the freedom to work whatever jobs she wished to work. She went to college. She later decided to come into business with me and Christale.

Keisha learned rapidly how to take care of pieces of business that help to keep cash flowing in. Christale trained Keisha, who helps to relieve some of Christale's responsibilities, because Christale's job is always expanding.

I was very glad to have Keisha end up here with us. When children step into your dream, it makes you that much more proud, that they think enough of it to support it. Keisha, you know, being single and being young, I felt that she also should be able to get a chance to be a part of this business and to learn as much as she can about running the place. Even if she decided at some point later to make other choices, no one could ever take away the knowledge she is getting at Michele Foods firsthand. In another business environment, she may have had to wait in line and would be lucky if she wound up in the short line for moving up quickly. A young woman her age is often a lady in waiting in corporate America. They wait and wait and wait and then they find that they were never equally considered for greater roles.

I always try to challenge my girls to find out if they have the makings for entrepreneurism. One day I told Keisha, "You know, you work for me, but you can have greater plans. You might want to go back to school and study business formally. Or maybe you want to study something else in detail."

I posed the question to her, "If I gave you some money to start something, what are you going to do with it?" I like to put thoughts like that into my daughters' minds.

I believe that you have to have something to call your very own. You have to have some type of vision for yourself. Too many times parents are inclined to give their children the fruits of their labor without giving them the foundation to support themselves and not squander their blessings. When parents are successful, and their children are under their shadow, some of us figure, "Okay, well, I'm going to pay you a salary to work for me. When I pay you, you can pay your rent and your car note and other bills. But if you need some extra money, fine. You know, you can always come to me. You can't pay your phone bill? Just put it on the company's tab."

But you can do just so much for your children. You don't want to handicap them with love and resources. It's tough. You're like, "Great, now I'm in a position to help." But you're really not helping because you turn around and you say, "Okay, what happens if I'm not here? What are you going to do?"

I want my girls to have an easy answer to those questions.

In Each Other's Hair

People ask what's it like to always be working with my daughters. It's great. It's wonderful. It's a blessing. And it's hard. I'm sure there is freedom in working for your mom, not having to be tied up in corporate politics, knowing that you have some flexibility, knowing that a part of this is yours walking in the door. There are advantages, true. But there are disadvantages, too. We don't always see eye to eye. We don't always do what the other expects. Sometimes this causes major conflict.

When we do break down, we break all the way down! When we break down and come at each other, it's explosive! I mean, it is something to see—and hear. It's like the ceiling has blown off the building. It doesn't happen a lot, but when it happens, it's never a minor occurrence. It's spectacular.

There's deep respect and love that I have for all of my girls, and they have for me. I mean, here are three girls that I've raised by myself and that I have—to let me tell it—sacrificed my life for. And so, I probably expect a little bit more out of them than a regular situation where you have a mom and dad—you know, your parents are a unit and you can go to either your daddy or your mama. But I've been Mama and Daddy to these girls, and I've also been the boss to them. To be the mother, father, and the boss is a tricky thing.

Honestly, when I think about it, I have ended up with a great relationship with my three daughters, even though it can become explosive. It's not, "Well, excuse me. I'm so sorry." It's like, "Boom! Boom!" Everything comes out. No matter the fight, though, I don't think that any of them could ever say that I was not a very attentive, providing mother. That has been my goal from day one; the responsibility of my daughters has been my motivation for the way I live, my spirituality, my work ethic, and my personality. That has been my center. My responsibility to them has always been at the core of my business pursuits.

From the time that I was told that I was having my first baby to the time that I went through labor to the time that I breastfed and carried them and took them to school and made sure they had Christmas presents, and all of it, equals to thirty-something years of everyday devotion. Sometimes I get really emotional about it, and I'll say to one of them, "Well, you know, you should treat me a little bit better." But these are individuals; these are people. They will have their own way of seeing things. And so I've had to transition from having babies and young little girls and young adults to dealing with grown women, and trying to define what the relationship should really be now that these are grown women and not little girls that I can buy dolls for and tell what to wear. (That's a whole other book!)

Everlasting Closeness

The thing about it is, you're never really grown with your mama because your mama can go back to when you weren't even here. She can go back to decisions she made to bring you here; the sacrifices she's made to raise you; the times when you've been sick with a high fever and she had to call the doctor and learn what to do; the responsibility of if you fall and skin your knee, she has to make it better; your first boyfriend and first date. The umbilical cord is never actually cut. It's always attached to you, even as an adult. It may be more emotional than physical, but it's always there.

Children grow up and become their own individuals and almost forget that their mother was their first everything. When you have a baby, you're with that child all the time. Every time that baby cries, you're often the first one that they see. You're always there. You're always attached. Who comes in and shows you how to detach this? Who steps in and says, "Okay, now she's twenty-one. Now this is the detachment phase. We're going to put this wall up. Just push her through to the other side, and your job is done"? So you have to really understand from a daughter's perspective and a child's perspective. How do you detach from your mother? And if you don't detach, how do you do it in a way that it's not going to be offensive or hurt her feelings or make her feel like all your work is in vain? A lot of mothers and daughters struggle with this. So have we. I once told Christale, "Christale, you cannot tell me how to detach from you or Keisha or Rosalyn if you've never had a child."

I think one of the problems we have in life is that there are no manuals for certain things that are the most important things here. There are no manuals for being a mother or being an entrepreneur. Whose word are you following? Whose guidelines? We're all looking for ways to follow. So you pull from the examples you've witnessed, and you act from those examples. But then you must reconsider the examples. Where were the people whose example you've followed when they were going through this similar situation? What time period did it happen? What was going on? It's a hard thing to do. It's life, though.

To be a mother, a father, and a boss to my girls has been the most difficult of things I've ever done. I mean, seriously. I think it would have been a little easier being the boss had I had a mate. Without a husband or a mate, I come home and all of my problems and my discussions are with my daughters. If someone's done something to me, I pick up the phone and I'm talking to them.

SUCCESS INGREDIENT THIRTY-SIX

Most of the most rewarding things in life—raising children, pursuing dreams—don't come with an instruction manual. You've got to make your own.

Chapter Thirty-Seven

My Rock

Few things can help an individual
more than to place responsibility on
him, and to let him know that you
trust him.

—*Booker T. Washington, educator,*
national leader

I LOVE ALL OF MY DAUGHTERS EQUALLY, but the one who has been my rock during the course of running Michele Foods has been Christale. She was my eyes when I was literally blind, so over the years I've learned to see things her way.

Christale is really the champion for me when it comes to Michele Foods. She stepped up to the plate eleven years ago, and has become my second in command. Without Christale, I would not have been as successful at this. She demonstrated early on just how much she really believed in this business. She has sacrificed her career goals, working for a little bit of money and a whole decade of her life to come and be a part of this.

When she came out of college, Christale had career plans. She wanted a career in the arts. She's very tall and graceful. She wanted to be an actress. She wanted to be a model. But she decided to come into the business with me. She helped me start this business when she was still at home with me, when she was still under my roof. But all the while, she had her individual interests and goals. But she stepped off her career track and helped her mother.

Tremendous Confidence

Christale's done a real transformation. She was living with me, going to work with me, coming home with me, the way Keisha is now. She was there when I started going through the brain tumor. So she's really been there for all the ups and downs of this whole journey. I have so much respect and appreciation for her. She has been my Girl Friday, my vice president, my secretary, and my financial person. She's really taken a lot of the load off of me so I can go out and be creative, and I can travel and I can go stand up and get an award and I can go to a city and stay a couple of days and meet with a buyer. I know she's back at the office making sure the phone is being answered and the mail is going out. She's making sure that the books are done. She's making sure that the p.o.'s are invoiced.

Christale didn't start off with a great salary. She started off having to understand that sometimes we don't get a paycheck. Sometimes we have to take our paycheck and pay a bill. And she understood that. So she allowed me to have some latitude. She did things that other people wouldn't have done. I pass everything in front of her. She watches my back when someone is trying to do something that isn't completely up front. She is always able to give me a different point of view.

When we moved from the crooked investor's office in LaGrange, Christale was carrying a computer to the car just like I was. When I got sick, she took care of the office. While I was at home recuperating for six weeks, she was at the office taking care of my business. And she was young doing these things. She was in her twenties. She's been here the whole while. She's never left. She's always been there. She's never left and gone and come back. She has been consistent; every day of her life for the last eleven years, she has helped me to run this business.

She's evolved into someone to whom I can go and say, "Girl . . . ," and she knows exactly what I mean. I could pick up the phone with her and I can almost say, "Yeah," and she can say, "I know what you mean." When she said to me, "Mama, you're going to be on *Oprah* someday," I said, "You know what? If you say it's going to happen, I believe it." And it happened. When she says these sort of things, I have enough faith and trust in her. She is like me—visionary. When she sat in the audience that first time, she was so happy for me, she cried.

Another day, she said, "You're going to be on there again." And it happened. She said a third time, "You're going to be on there again." And it happened. Every time that happened, we gave ourselves a high-five. Those are very special moments for us.

Whenever she gives me her thoughts on a matter, I know that she is pure in saying it. She doesn't have any ulterior motive for saying, "You're qualified to do that, Mama. I believe that you are." Maybe love is an ulterior motive, but I'd take that over someone who is obviously motivated by profit. Sometimes, the truth is, I didn't believe I was qualified for something just yet. But she believed. Because she believed I was, I believed I was.

Trust

One thing about my daughters that I am certain of: I can trust them. I know they've got my back. That's a feeling everybody should have about someone. But it's not a given for everyone. So I know that I am blessed.

After some early lapses in control and judgment, I have never known how it would feel or be to have someone handle my money because Christale always has. If the check is $1 or a check is $10,000, I can give it to her and I've never, ever had to worry about that. I've never had to worry about a p.o. She takes care of my business. It's just never been a worry. And I think, I could probably appreciate that more had I had that problem.

And I did have that situation somewhat with that investor because we didn't handle the money then, and it wasn't a pretty outcome. So I've vowed that either I or my daughter will write and sign the checks. She signs them. She's on my bank account. She's the one that's my cosigner. She's my secondary person. She's Mini-Me. She's never come to me and said, "You know what? I can't do this." She's told me a multitude of times, "This is your dream, not mine," but she's never left me; she's never abandoned me. Things have come up that were challenging.

She does get chances to step out and be creative and do the things she wants to do. Christale has performed in local stage productions. But she also puts Michele Foods first. I don't know if she knows the magnitude of what she has learned to do. I bought my house the same year I had the brain problem. I moved into my house a month after I had my surgery. I was close to incapacitated. So Christale had to do all of the paperwork. When she bought her own home, she didn't have to blink—she'd learned it all from my buying a home.

It's the same thing with her taking care of the business. Christale can run a company because she knows how to run mine. And I think that's a great lesson for her, the stuff of the legacy. I can step away from this business, and I can go on vacation and I can go to a conference or I could go on a sales trip and everything is fine. There's never been any major problem that Christale could not handle.

I really appreciate all of her advice. She'll give me advice that, had I followed it, I would not have had the problem that I had to begin with. She'll say, "Well, you know, I told you so." A lot of times she'll be trying to tell me something and I'll be very stubborn. I'll say, "No, no, I'm going to do this my way!" When I look up, my way was the wrong way and her way was the right way. Then I have had to go back and say, "Yeah,

Christale, you were right." So now I know there's value in listening to her. There have been times when she's told me not to sign a contract, and I signed it, and it's been the worst thing I could have done. Or she'll tell me, "You know, I don't trust this person," and I'll be like, "No, no, they're okay." And she's been right. She has great natural instincts.

A Fresh Perspective

I think Christale's been right when I've been wrong due to the fact that we come from different vantage points in seeing the business. Because she's second in command, she's not under the emotion that I might be under. I might be under certain emotions because I really want this help and I really want this to be the right person. And I really need it right now, and I really want this to happen right now. So this has got to be the right time and the right person because I drew them to me. Then with her, it's not so imminent. She's not under that pressure of saying, "Well, if this doesn't happen now, I'm going to have to exert a little bit more energy," or "I'm going to have to do something else that puts it into play," or "I've been looking for this type of person, so please let this be the person." She's not under that pressure.

Christale also doesn't take this home with her in the same way that I do, which is a good thing. She does not need that pressure. I mean, she takes it home to some degree, but it's like the head chief and the co-chief. The head chief is the one who's going to sit up looking for the foxes. The co-chief knows the head chief is looking for the foxes. It's, "I'll look for the foxes when you're not there, but most of the time you're looking for the foxes, so I know that I can rest." I think that saves her nerves and saves her ability to figure things out at a slower rate than I do.

I'm under a different level of pressure. I'm the one out here running to and fro to find new business. I'm the captain, and the captain is the one who's going to stay up the extra twelve hours. The captain's going to be the one who's going to miss meals. You take the co-captain, and you make sure that she eats and she rests so that when the captain is weary, the co-captain is strong enough to do the job.

So Christale's always got some kind of reserved energy because whereas she might say, "Well, okay, I'm leaving at 5 P.M.," I'm saying, "Okay, I'll be here until 8." She doesn't necessarily have to stay there until 8 P.M. It's not that kind of pressure on her. She can do her job tomorrow. But I've got to do mine right now. So when I'm exhausted, she has the reserve to come in and say, "Okay, great, since I haven't stayed until 8 P.M. for the last twelve days, I can stay until 8 P.M. tonight." It's not always her responsibility, but she is able to step up to the plate because she understands the job.

SUCCESS INGREDIENT THIRTY-SEVEN

A true partner is someone you can trust absolutely and at all times.

Chapter Thirty-Eight

Keeper of Tradition

When you tell a story you automatically talk
about traditions, but they're never separate
from the people, the human implications.
You're talking about your connections as a
human being.

—Gayle Jones, novelist

M Y MOTHER, AUDREY RUSSELL, and I have a special relationship, too. We have been through a lot together,
some good times and some not so good times. I am my
mother's only daughter, and sometimes I think that fact alone
has made for days of contention. I was the one where she
probably expected to see more of a reflection of herself. But I
was always different. Over time, she has learned to accept and
respect that. She has looked past her expectations and finally
seen the real me, which is what I'd always craved.

The rest of my family has followed suit. It feels good to
be able to talk about how encouraging my family has become,
about how proud my mother is now. My mother was afraid

early on that the world would end up with the secret recipe. She thought I was going to just give it away. But I've proven that was never my intention. My intention was to use the recipe to obtain strength—for myself, for our family, for our race, for other women. Giving it away would have been like giving away a gold mine.

My mother has learned that I know better than that. There are telling moments nowadays that are filled with the emotion of what we've all come through. We often get misty-eyed together. It might be something small that sets us off. I showed my mother and my daughters an ad that ran in the *Chicago Sun-Times* during Black History Month. It was just an ad where consumers could buy two bottles of syrup for $5. But the ad had a little picture of me, and it had a little caption. On this day, I was over at my mom's house, and they were throwing the garbage out. I saw the newspaper, and I pulled it out of the trash. I said, "Y'all didn't see me in the paper?" And they were like, "Oh?!" They didn't know it was there. When they saw the ad, they started crying and hugging me. I'm thinking, "Wow, it's just an ad!"

Precious Evolution

But that moment had the emotion of twenty years in it. My family evolved from "You're in the basement, and you're not going to be able to pull this off" to being my biggest allies. I marvel now at how proud they were when they saw me on *Oprah* and how proud they were when my mother, Christale, and I were pictured in *People* magazine. I sometimes think about how upsetting it was that I did not get early support. But now I, too, understand.

If you tell your mother, "I'm getting ready to stop working and start a company," and you have no clue how to go about such a thing, how would she react? Parents tend to feel that at some point they want you to be secure and they want you to be productive and when you stop and go in a direction different from what they anticipate, they hold on to what they know. Many parents, especially from the old school, don't understand an entrepreneurial route. They don't know that they've raised this type of person. That is—my father always knew he had raised this type of person. My mother didn't know. I can go to my father and say, "I'm getting ready to run across the George Washington Bridge," and he'll say, "What kind of shoes do you need?" But my mother'll be like, "Oh, my God! You're going to trip and fall. You're going to fall over in the water. Oh, my God! This is going to end the world. Why don't you just be still and raise a family." The early days of this journey were a real stretch for my mother. But now that I've done it, like everyone else in my family, she is like, "Okay, great. We really support what you do next." She's proud and that makes me even more proud.

Single Mom

Through the whole course of this book, I haven't talked about a man other than my ex-husband. There hasn't been one in my life. I used to struggle with that. I used to really struggle with being single. I was taught that you've just got to have a man in your life. And even though I stepped out on my own and declared my independence, it's hard to go against the tide of what you were raised to believe. My mama and daddy have been married sixty-something years, and they're still in love and they're still together. That's remarkable. But I just realized in the last three or four years that it's not a real necessity to be part of a couple. What I've learned is, once you become happy with yourself and you know who you are, you don't look for anything outside of that.

I knew early on that with my divorce and my being very focused on business that it could be challenging to find myself in a relationship that worked with my entrepreneurial goals. I think with me being the type of woman that I am, I would probably have not been as successful if I had a man in my life.

I was taught to be subservient to a man. I was taught that a man was the most important thing for a woman to have, and that would mean that my business would have to take a back seat to a relationship. If I had fallen in love or really become committed to a man, I would have had to split my commitment to this business and share it with him. I could not be this way.

Because I didn't have that in my life, I put a lot of energies into business. Plus, I had to know that I could take care of my daughters and myself. I have built this mountain of security by myself such that I don't feel insecure about not having a man at all. I don't have the fear of, "Oh, my God. If I divorce him, where am I going to live?" Most women who are like me—

mature women who have accomplished great things singularly—are some of the most secure women you're ever going to meet. For some guys, we can be a bit intimidating. Maybe that's why I've looked up and twenty years later, and here I am still single. If it must be, then so be it, I say.

But I'm not antirelationship. I'm just saying that it's not the end of the world if you're not in one. I would love for it to happen! But it's not something I'm going around pining for. I'm not trying to go on the Internet to find a man or go to a dating service. I think that now I'm at a point in my life where I can sit down and enjoy a relationship, but it probably would have to be with someone to whom I could relate on a business level, someone who understands my level of commitment to my business. It might have to be somebody who is a peer of mine. But it doesn't actually *have* to be anybody at all.

SUCCESS INGREDIENT THIRTY-EIGHT

Building success the hard way makes you appreciate it even more.

Chapter Thirty-Nine

Good People

If I have someone who believes in
me, I can move mountains.

—*Diana Ross, soul superstar*

PEOPLE HAVE PLAYED SOME VERY DRAMATIC ROLES in my evolution as a businesswoman. I've mentioned situations in which people were shape shifters who turned out to be someone other than who they presented themselves to be. At times, I've been very gullible and naive while growing up with my business. I've been betrayed on a few occasions. I talked about these incidents because they contain important lessons that I wanted to share. My thought was that maybe somebody out there could learn from my mistakes. You may be in a similar place—passionate and determined to accomplish a goal with very little knowledge of what you're doing.

But not everyone was out to take advantage of me. So I must give credit, too, where credit is due. I've met many, many people who have been kind, generous, honest, helpful, and upstanding. These people have done a great deal for me.

I've found that it's true what my daughter Christale has said. She once pointed out to me that every time someone comes into your life who is not 100 percent genuine, when you close the door behind that person, you may find another one opens up to a more sincere individual. Behind that door might be a genuine friend or advocate.

The Early Days

I remember in the days before I started the business, I wanted to find out what some respected business-minded people thought of the idea. So I had a breakfast at my home one morning in 1982, and I invited a few local business-people I knew. Two key people who came to that breakfast were Don Jackson, who is now president of Central City Productions, a local television production company, and the late Frank Brooks, who would later become a meat manu-facturer with McDonald's as a major client. They tasted the syrup, and I told them how I really wanted to put it on the market. They're among the very few who encouraged me early on to go for my dream, no matter what the odds seemed to be.

I asked Frank about running a business, and if he thought it would be a difficult thing. He, in his entrepre-neurial spirit, told me that entrepreneurs were unique individ-uals, risk takers, and that those are some of the components that were necessary for success. He said that he thought I had those traits.

Don also particularly encouraged me. After I started the business, Don was the first person who thought enough of my story then to give me some media exposure. The ink had barely dried on the incorporation papers for Michele Foods then. It was brand new; it wasn't even warm yet, and he put me on his TV show and gave me some exposure. He popped up periodically in my life after that, and I don't think he and I even realized it. The next time I ran across Don at a major event, he presented me with an entrepreneurial award. Who would have thought that when he was sitting at my breakfast table in 1982, I'd be standing on a stage getting an award from him? I always remember that whenever I see Don. Since then, I've been featured several times on his show, *Minority Business Report*.

I also received encouragement and early support from Hedy Ratner, founder and co-president of the Women's Business Development Center in downtown Chicago. When I first started out, after I left Marshall Field's, I went over to the Women's Business Development Center and met Hedy. She took me by my hand and took me right over to the Thompson Center, where she helped me to get the paperwork started to establish my business. She also made certain to introduce me to key people in city government. I've never forgotten her dedication.

Magaly Petersen-Penn, who was director of minority development for Flagstar, then parent company of Denny's, was very forthcoming in giving me useful information that helped me grow as a businesswoman. I went down to Greensville, North Carolina, and met with her on a Denny's matter and she encouraged me to join Women's Foodservice Forum, which was founded in 1989 to support advancement of executive women in the foodservice industry. I joined the organization in 1997, and have since been an active member. Women's Foodservice Forum is a wonderful organization, and I have been taken into their fold with open arms. In 2003, I was nominated and appointed to be on their board of directors. There are some terrific women on this board, and it's given me the opportunity to really get to know them. These relationships stretch you. They stretch your abilities. They stretch your knowledge.

The Last Decade

I made one of my most rewarding friendships and business advocates in the powder room! I was at conference in the Washington, D.C., area when I met publisher Jamie Foster Brown. She founded and publishes *Sister2Sister* magazine. The event was an empowerment forum for black women, and a gentleman I knew introduced us. Later, we got up and went to the bathroom at the same time and came out friends. She featured me in the magazine, and I pick up the phone and call her and we talk, and whenever she's in town we hang out.

Jamie's sister, Stella Foster, is now a columnist with the *Chicago Sun-Times* after spending many years working alongside Irv Kupcinet, a legendary figure in Chicago journalism who died in November 2003. Whenever I had news of some new milestone with Michele Foods, Stella would always make certain that it was in Kup's column.

Pat Harris, who is the Chief Diversity Officer for McDonald's Corporation, is among my closest friends. Pat has been at McDonald's almost thirty years, and she has really taken diversity to another level. McDonald's is an organization that is very diverse and values its employees throughout the organization. She's always been an inspiration to me.

Authors Hattie Hill, who wrote that book *Smart Women, Smart Choices*, and Cheryl Broussard, who runs her own money-management business and who wrote the book *Sister CEO: The Black Woman's Guide to Starting Her Own Business*, are friends and very intelligent women to whom I can turn for information and advice.

I would also like to acknowledge Vicki Scurlock-Bunn, president of Diversity Food Management, Inc. She and I have been friends for ten years, and I have a lot of respect for her and the work she does. She's one of the reasons I was able to meet and develop a business relationship with Ed McManus, president of Cub Foods, Eastern Region. He is a wonderful gentleman who is very committed to the diversity programs within the Cub Foods/SuperValu family.

I also am indebted to Hala Moddelmog, who as president of Church's Chicken is one of the highest-ranking women in the quick-service restaurant industry, and Frank Belatti, president of Church's parent AFC, who went to bat for me so that I could win business with their organization. They were my protectors when that opportunity was threatened. Today, I'm doing condiments for Church's Chicken because of their generosity in wanting to support my business.

And then there's Bishop Arthur Brazier, pastor of Apostolic Church of God. When I had the brain tumor, I would go in and sit in his office and he would pray with me and anoint me with oil. He sent the prayer angels to my hospital bed and that was really important to me. Then when I was on the front page of *N'Digo*, a local African-American-owned publication, he told the whole congregation about it. He said, "We've got one of our members on the cover of *N'Digo*," and he put the paper up and everybody saw it.

SUCCESS INGREDIENT THIRTY-NINE

You succeed on your own. But the support of good people is essential in your journey.

Chapter Forty

Stomping for the Cause

Service to others is the rent you pay
for your room here on earth.

—*Muhammad Ali, boxer*

OVER THE YEARS, I HAVE RACKED UP quite a few frequent-flier miles traipsing about the country speaking about my business. One of my most memorable speaking engagements was the keynote address I made to the graduating class of Johnson & Wales University in 2002.

I was the first African-American woman to speak at a commencement exercise for a graduating student body. It was a blessing to stand before those college graduates and received such a distinction.

To top it off, I was awarded an honorary doctorate degree. That was a grand occasion for me. When you get an honorary doctor's degree, they give you the cap and gown. That was pretty special. I've come a long way as a speaker since my first speaking engagement, which will always loom large in my mind.

224

Learning from My First

The first time I spoke about my experiences in building Michele Foods was in 1996 at the *Black Enterprise* Entrepreneurs Conference. The magazine, which speaks to black professionals, families, and consumers about money and business, had selected me to receive its Emerging Company of the Year Award. When *Black Enterprise* called me, it was the first time that anyone had called me and said, "We think you're qualified enough to come to speak to other entrepreneurs about business." I was really excited about that.

So when they asked me to be a part of a panel discussion and to prepare a presentation on cash flow, I said, "Okay, yeah, sure. I know about cash flow." I didn't know anything about cash flow! But I happily agreed to participate in any way that they wanted me.

Later, I got very nervous about agreeing to the presentation. Cash flow is something that accountants teach. But I had agreed, and so I had to do it. Just as I have done in business, I had to figure it out after the fact.

I spent a month learning about cash flow. I had charts and graphs. I had my researched facts. I made transparencies. Oh, honey, I had this thing down pat! I had to make it remarkable. I would be on a panel with some of the top accountants, bankers, and financiers in the country. Plus, conference organizers were very accommodating. The event was being held at Disney World in Orlando, Florida. I had never, ever in all my lifetime taken my kids to Disney World. And I was able to take my two daughters, Christale and Keisha, down with me, all expenses paid. They gave me unlimited everything.

My Speech

I was really excited because it was the week of May 12. Keisha had just turned twenty-one.

We were down there for three days. We stayed in this wonderful hotel. We were able to experience all of this and celebrate her birthday. But there was business to tend to.

When it was nearing time for me to speak, I was really, really nervous. I was in front of 2,000 African-American movers and shakers. These were 2,000 dynamic people who had come down to this conference with a purpose. They had paid money for this conference, and they were expecting to learn something. And I was really thinking about that. My hands were wet and shaky. Christale was in the front row. And I had a couple of friends in the audience who had come to the conference, and they were in the front row. Thank goodness that I really couldn't see the rest of the audience—once they dim the lights, you're lucky to see your panel mates.

They introduced the other panelists one by one. Then when it was my turn to speak, they said, "Here's Michele Hoskins, CEO of Michele Foods." I got up with my perspiration-slicked hands and as I walked up the steps to the podium, I had a change of heart. There was a wastepaper basket right beside the stage, and I dropped the whole presentation in the garbage. When I got to the microphone, I said, "I don't want to talk about that." People were like, "Oh, my God!" I said, "I want to talk about what I understand, and what cash flow means to me." And I started talking about my business and how I got started and about when I first went into this buyer's office with my one bottle of product and how my great-great-grandmother had been born a slave but came up with this wonderful syrup recipe and that it found its way into my hands and I dared to start a business with it. And as I started talking about this, I started crying and it was really emotional. But I couldn't stop. I talked about having had the brain tumor, and barely surviving it three years earlier.

After I was done speaking, none of the other panelists would follow me. They didn't want to hear anything else. The panelists said, "We don't have anything to say." I got a standing ovation. After that, throngs of people came up to me saying, "That was so inspiring. May I have your business card, please."

That was one of my most esteemed speaking experiences, and it was the first.

SUCCESS INGREDIENT FORTY

If you tell your story from your heart, people will respond.

Chapter Forty-One

Sharing Knowledge with Others

When you learn, teach.
When you get, give.
—*Maya Angelou, writer*

I DON'T ALWAYS THROW OUT THE CHARTS and the graphs. They've got their place, such as in my mentoring activities.

I have had some successful relationships where I've mentored or taught women entrepreneurs how to get their products out there in the marketplace. One woman is a member of my church and she put a bottled iced tea out there. She was among the first that I assisted. It was something that I marveled at. Here was someone coming into my office, starting from scratch like I was twenty years ago. She was interested in my story as a way to inform the process she was about to go through, and so, I showed her how to do what she wanted, just basing it all on my experiences.

I shared what I had learned and told her how to do it. I was able to explain to her that you can't make a product from your home because the ingredients that you're using already have been retailed. Then later, I was able to find her a co-packer. So I had to take her through all of those things. I was pleasantly surprised that I was able to teach her so much. I didn't even know how much I knew until I started teaching someone else.

Sharing My Success

Later, I helped Calvita Frederick-Sowell put her Magnolia Spice Teas on the market through my mentoring program. I also helped a friend named Amy Hilliard understand the process of developing a product for the retail market. She now has a wonderful line of cakes on the market called Comfort-Cakes.

These were all African-American women, walking into my office, starting bravely with little knowledge just like I was twenty years ago. I had no one, so I'm glad that they had me. I was happy to be able to in some way help them fulfill their dreams. With hindsight about my own business, I could see that you don't always have to spend money to move forward to the next steps. Truth be told, I didn't have to spend $150,000 to do what I did. I've realized that you don't even need to have much money to start a company. You need to have some, but that isn't the only determining factor as to whether or not it will work.

Recipe to Retail

So a lot of people have asked me to help them, and as best I could, I have answered the call. Some had the spirit that I had early on, and some didn't. The proof is always in the pudding. (No, none of them wanted to put pudding on the market!)

I like mentoring, but it's not as easy as people think, because when you mentor someone in an industry that has few information resources, you have nowhere else to send them. You can't mentor somebody and say, "Okay, well, go take this course." Then it becomes very time-consuming. I would have people calling me all the time. I wanted to help these people, but I didn't have enough time to take care of my own business. So what I did was, I started combining mentoring with classes. I charged a fee for the classes and limited the time I could interact with aspiring entrepreneurs to six sessions. But I would see them for six consecutive weeks, and we would meet six to eight times during those weeks. That's all I felt it took.

Eventually, as the calls became more consistent, I decided to do classes. I authored a curriculum called Recipe to Retail and authored a class textbook of the same title to use with my class.

The classes drew budding entrepreneurs from all over the country. I taught and mentored them. These interactions started them on the process of getting food products on the market. Mentoring is a very satisfying thing, but it's *very* time-consuming. With me running my own business, it got to the point where I was spending perhaps too much time doing that. But I was very dedicated to giving back. I wanted to make sure that the people who wanted to do this had more resources than I had when I came into the food industry.

Birds of a Feather

Being an entrepreneur can be an isolating pursuit. In addition to mentoring, I have found that joining with like-minded and like-spirited individuals through associations and organizations is a way to offset the isolation, to learn from peers, and to share knowledge. Over the years, I have been involved with several associations and organizations. As I mentioned, I have worked with Operation PUSH's Food Spoke, an organization where minority food retailers meet once a month to exchange ideas and network, and Women's Foodservice Forum.

I am also a member of Multicultural Foodservice and Hospitality Alliance, founded and chaired by Gerry Fernandez. I was Gerry's very first member. I signed up before he had even organized the alliance. Gerry suggested that I be considered for the honorary doctorate at Johnson & Wales.

My group affiliations are very important to me. They're like little pep pills. They help to create relationships. They're great for networking. They help you to position yourself in your industry. Good group affiliations are key to any occupation. In businesses such as the one I'm in, they are a resource for oh-so-crucial networking, which is just phenomenal. Just showing up helps you to be in the right place at the right time when it comes to effective networking. It gives you opportunities.

To give you an example, I was at a conference one year in Dallas, the Women's Foodservice Forum conference. We had just gotten the business with Denny's, and it was a very exciting time. I was sitting at Denny's table. At that table, a woman by the name of Edna Morris sat across from me. She was president of Coco's and Carrows, two restaurant chains under the umbrella of Denny's parent company, Advantica (the name Flagstar took in 1998). After she took her seat across the table from me, we were introduced to each other. I explained to her that I made pancake syrup and had just started in on a deal with Denny's to provide syrup for the restaurants. She looked across at me and asked, "Well, why aren't you making syrup for our restaurants?"

Later that evening we went to this wonderful, huge barn dance. We had our cowboy boots on, and we rode the mechanical bull. In fact, Edna and myself and several other ladies rode this mechanical bull together. And we just kind of bonded. Edna went on to become the president of Red Lobster, and she still is a great friend of mine. And she's still a business acquaintance. Whenever we see each other, we are really ecstatic. I think the feeling is mutual about our friendship. So joining relevant associations is important. I mean, how many people meet the president of a Red Lobster?

Another important contact that I met at an industry event is Lloyd L. Hill, CEO and president of Applebee's. He and I were on a panel together at a Women's Foodservice Forum event. I've met some really wonderful people. Meeting

Lloyd Hill was like meeting a celebrity to someone like me. I mean, these are people whose restaurants are fixtures of the American landscape. You ride past their restaurants and you never know who sits at the head of these large corporations and to be able to meet people such as them, it's just a really good experience. It gives you a really good network and it gives you a really good Rolodex.

So networking is very important. That's why I believe in organizations, serving on boards, speaking for organizations—because it always pays off, sometimes in unexpected ways. You always meet people, have doors opened to you, open doors for others. People remember you, and you remember people. It personalizes people in your industry. You get to know who they are. When your work is exceptional, you may even get accolades from these peers when they honor your efforts and accomplishments as an entrepreneur. The Phenomenal Woman Award, the *Dollars and Sense* awards, the Entrepreneur of the Year Award, and the honorary doctorate degree—these are things that have been bestowed on me because of the relationships I've developed and because of my involvement in a network and in organizations that I support enthusiastically. These have all been rewarding experiences.

SUCCESS INGREDIENT FORTY-ONE

Find your professional community—you will get support and learning and fun from it.

Chapter Forty-Two

Evolution

No matter how far a person can go
the horizon is still way beyond you.
                    —*Zora Neale Hurston, author*

I'M RIGHT AT A POINT WHERE I can say, "Been there, done that" with so many things in this industry. I've done the starting of the company part. I've experienced the growth of the company. I've experienced incredible growth as an individual and as an entrepreneur. I've overcome twenty years' worth of obstacles.

But my life didn't start twenty years ago, although it definitely got more interesting. And it's not ending just because I'm twenty years into this and I feel that I've accomplished so much. Twenty years is not my entire life. I'm just at a point now in my life where I'm figuring out who I really am, but I have a whole other journey that I want to venture into. I know Michele Foods is in capable hands, and I'm still involved in it, but I have raised really capable daughters and staff. So I can step out and do other things, such as write a book, mentor new people, and maybe speak more about my experiences.

New Horizons

But even with those things, there's more that I want for Michele Foods. I'm not looking for an exit plan, but an entrance plan and to what lies in the future. Where do I take this experience? And where do I go? I want to continue to grow Michele Foods, but grow it where it becomes a household name. It's almost like you birth a child and the child grows up and goes to college and becomes somebody. And so, I gave birth to Michele Foods. I've raised Michele Foods. But I need to turn Michele Foods over to the world in order for it to really live up to its potential. It's time for everyone to know about it. That's the new challenge. We have to figure out how to position Michele's syrups to become as commonly known as Mrs. Butterworth's, as Hungry Jack, as Log Cabin, and all the others. And I'm still trying to figure it all out. But that's where I'm trying to go with this.

There was a time when I was saying, "I wonder what's my exit plan? What do I do? Do I retire and go somewhere and buy a home in Florida and learn how to fish or play golf? Or do I reinvent my entrepreneurial spirit and just do something else?" But I'm not looking for an exit plan right now.

I have taken this particular company as far as I can go without a different model. It's almost like learning everything there is to know about swimming—while you are swimming!

You get through ponds, then streams, then lakes, and then rivers. But when you get to the edge of the ocean, you realize that in order to get to the other side alive, you may need somebody with a boat.

Ready and Willing

Through all of this I've realized that this is something that I cannot do alone. My plan will have to accommodate for the involvement of outsiders, which can be scary, given some of the ways I've been burned in the past.

But if that's what it takes to grow, so be it. I am ready this time. This is what I have to do for Michele Foods to become a household name. It will take a different model than the one I've got. It will take marketing and advertising. It will take a whole lot of other things. It may take being under the umbrella of a larger company. It may take a deal such as the one where Orville Redenbacher sold his popcorn company to a conglomerate but hung around as the face of the company. Either way, I plan to be a presence. I am Michele Foods, and Michele Foods is me.

SUCCESS INGREDIENT FORTY-TWO

The journey to success is never-ending, because success is not a single destination. Loving the journey is success in itself.

Afterword

by Christale Gray

MY MOTHER IS SIMPLY AWESOME. How many kids do you hear say that? Well, I'm not a kid anymore. I am all grown up now, with plenty of confidence, ability, and business know-how, all thanks to my mother.

I didn't always recognize just how awesome she is. Back when she was making syrup down in my grandmother's basement, I was in my early teen years, and I wasn't involved much. I didn't really comprehend what my mother was trying to do. I just thought, "This is a mess!"

But as I got older, I started to appreciate my mother's nerve. I put two and two together and said, "Okay, she's really trying to build something here." I became interested in her struggle to turn the syrup into a business. She was working really hard. I started helping out, taking the syrup around to stores and trying to sell it right alongside her. Those are sweet memories. But just like the syrup she's built her name on, this journey has been at times both sweet and sticky.

My most vivid memories begin when I started working for her full-time, which was about eleven years ago. Those were the sticky years. There was lots of struggle, but my mother was really determined to grow her brand. It was when she manufactured the two other flavors, Maple Crème and Butter Pecan, that it really hit home that this is really going somewhere. This can really flourish.

Witnessing her struggle and the outcome of her efforts has been an inspiration to me on so many levels. It made me try my best to learn the food business. For a long time, there was just the two of us running the business. We did what we had to do. I started out doing whatever was necessary, really, from packing boxes to placing orders for raw materials to making sales calls. Sometimes I would have to go to the city and deliver the product. If I had to do a product demo, then I would do it. I shipped things out to brokers. I helped to write the checks. I helped to balance the books. I've done it all.

There were times when we didn't have much money coming in, but I stuck in there because I believed in my mother. I still do. She's always been very determined. Whatever she's done, she's always gone straight for the top with it. She always had this entrepreneur's spirit.

I was working in retail at Sears when I decided to leave and work with my mother. It was a period of transition. Sears was offering buyouts to trim back. My choices were to stay with the company and move up, move to another location, or take the buyout. My mother said, "Chris, come and work for me."

I chose to go with her because I always thought that she was this person who got the job done. She was single with three kids, and she always made it work. We always had things. We were never so poor that we couldn't get at least some of the things that we wanted. She always made things happen.

She's always instilled in all of us, "You can do whatever you want to do. You don't have to take no for an answer. You don't have to settle." So I figured, "Why stay here at Sears and be limited?" I could help her out and at the same time grow with her. I didn't really know where we would end up, but I had the confidence that it would be someplace special.

I remember when she almost lost the business to an unscrupulous investor. She kept asking me, "What should I do? What should I do?" That time was so strange, but I said, "You know what? We can make it. We can really make it on our own."

I felt like as long as she had me and I had her, we could do it. We were pretty much running it anyway. It was her business, so she knew it inside and out. Plus, I had learned a lot, and I'm not dumb by far. So I told her, "What would keep us from succeeding?" We wouldn't have this authority-type figure over us and we wouldn't have the cushion of his financial backing. But we took a chance that we could make it nevertheless.

The toughest days of my time working with my mother were when she was going through her medical crisis. That showed me what I was made of. I had to be there for her to lean on—to be what she had always been for the business. It was hard to see my mother, the strongest woman I knew, fighting for her life. We had never been through anything like that in our family. My mother gave me power of attorney, and I had to stay strong for her. She had put her heart and soul into Michele Foods, and I was not going to let it fall apart. I had to do things that I had never even known about.

I was very young, and it was scary. But my mother had trained me well, just by her example. So I told myself, "Right now, you just have to put on your game face and whatever your mother needs you to do, you've got to do it—whether it be to hold her hand while she goes to the doctor and hear about this diagnosis or answer the phones and take charge where she can't right now." It was really hard on me, but I got through it.

If it were not for my mother, I don't think I would be the person that I am today. I believe honestly that I can do anything just from witnessing what she's done. This woman actually took a quaint family recipe and turned it into a multimillion-dollar business. I look at Michele's Syrups twenty years later, and our success just amazes me. How many African-American people have a product in major retail stores across the country? How many women have done that? How many welfare moms have done that?

I feel that I'm blessed to be able to say that my mother is my role model. She is the woman who raised me. I saw her do the impossible. When I'm trying to get something done, I think, "What would my mother do?" I've learned some great things from her. I've learned how to set goals. I've learned how to go about achieving those goals and never stopping until I actually accomplish those goals. My mother showed me how important it is to take emotion and the personal stuff out of the equation and just concentrate on business. If it's for the good of business, it's for the good of business.

Like my mother, I have big dreams for Michele Foods. I will always be a part of the company because I am very proud of it. I am so grateful to have such a wonderful mother. I'm in awe of her. Someday, I'll sit on the board of directors and continue to help guide the company's direction. Although the road to success hasn't always been easy, I wouldn't change one single lesson I've learned through it all.

Michele's Ingredients for Success

SUCCESS INGREDIENT ONE

Be open to change, and be ready to embrace it—change can wreak havoc on your life, but it can also bring you life's greatest gifts.

SUCCESS INGREDIENT TWO

Be ready to listen to *eureka* moments. The most unexpected sources can show you the way to transform your life and create your own destiny.

SUCCESS INGREDIENT THREE

Sometimes the key to your success is right in front of you—sometimes it's something that you've known since you were a little child.

SUCCESS INGREDIENT FOUR

Find the right people to help you on your journey—and be patient with those who might be resistant at first. They can't always see your vision.

SUCCESS INGREDIENT FIVE

The best way to reach people—whether you're selling something, or teaching something, or motivating someone to do their best work—is to listen and learn to see a situation from their point of view.

SUCCESS INGREDIENT SIX

Find the people who will inspire you to realize your own potential, and listen well.

SUCCESS INGREDIENT SEVEN

Passion, patience, and perseverance will make up for what you don't have in money—but no amount of money will make up for not having all three Ps.

SUCCESS INGREDIENT EIGHT

If you fight with everything you've got, you'll come out on top.

SUCCESS INGREDIENT NINE

Hard work pays off when you watch for opportunities and have the determination to grab them.

SUCCESS INGREDIENT TEN

Sometimes a little success can have a lot of consequences at first—but the education you gain is worth the cost.

SUCCESS INGREDIENT ELEVEN

Watch out for the limitations you put on yourself—they can be just as confining as the ones other people put on you.

SUCCESS INGREDIENT TWELVE

Carve out your identity and make it work for you.

SUCCESS INGREDIENT THIRTEEN

Be grateful for the good fortune that's given you whatever measure of success you've won thus far—and fight like hell to keep it.

SUCCESS INGREDIENT FOURTEEN

Do whatever it takes to recover from a setback, and always keep faith.

SUCCESS INGREDIENT FIFTEEN

Opportunity will only knock if you're persistent and motivated.

SUCCESS INGREDIENT SIXTEEN

Taking any endeavor to the next level is thrilling and demanding.

SUCCESS INGREDIENT SEVENTEEN

Sometimes life gives you the worst and the best it has—right at the same time.

SUCCESS INGREDIENT EIGHTEEN

Only faith can carry you through the hardest stuff life can throw at you.

SUCCESS INGREDIENT NINETEEN

Life's worst blows can show you something important.

SUCCESS INGREDIENT TWENTY

Health comes before business and before everything else.

SUCCESS INGREDIENT TWENTY-ONE

Everyone must feed himself or herself spiritually.

SUCCESS INGREDIENT TWENTY-TWO

Never let other people's expectations get in the way of your own expectations for yourself.

SUCCESS INGREDIENT TWENTY-THREE

You control your own destiny.

SUCCESS INGREDIENT TWENTY-FOUR

Take risks to reach your goals.

SUCCESS INGREDIENT TWENTY-FIVE

Success does not make you immune to attack.

SUCCESS INGREDIENT TWENTY-SIX

It's always worth it to take the high road—but that doesn't mean it won't be costly.

SUCCESS INGREDIENT TWENTY-SEVEN

There's always something good to be gained out of a tough situation.

SUCCESS INGREDIENT TWENTY-EIGHT

You're never too important to stir the pot yourself—be willing to do what you have to do.

SUCCESS INGREDIENT TWENTY-NINE

A tough situation can be an opportunity for valuable learning.

SUCCESS INGREDIENT THIRTY

If you believe you can do anything, you can—and you will.

SUCCESS INGREDIENT THIRTY-ONE

Your own creativity can make up a lot for money you don't have.

SUCCESS INGREDIENT THIRTY-TWO

Staying connected to your community is a source of strength.

SUCCESS INGREDIENT THIRTY-THREE

A good role model will elevate you: She has a magical effect.

SUCCESS INGREDIENT THIRTY-FOUR

Trust yourself and your own experience. Be your own best support.

SUCCESS INGREDIENT THIRTY-FIVE

Give thanks for the precious support that you have.

SUCCESS INGREDIENT THIRTY-SIX

Most of the most rewarding things in life—raising children, pursuing dreams—don't come with an instruction manual. You've got to make your own.

SUCCESS INGREDIENT THIRTY-SEVEN

A true partner is someone you can trust absolutely and at all times.

SUCCESS INGREDIENT THIRTY-EIGHT

Building success the hard way makes you appreciate it even more.

SUCCESS INGREDIENT THIRTY-NINE

You succeed on your own. But the support of good people is essential in your journey.

SUCCESS INGREDIENT FORTY

If you tell your story from your heart, people will respond.

SUCCESS INGREDIENT FORTY-ONE

Find your professional community—you will get support and learning and fun from it.

SUCCESS INGREDIENT FORTY-TWO

The journey to success is never-ending, because success is not a single destination. Loving the journey is success in itself.

Index

About the Author

MICHELE HOSKINS is the founder and owner of Michele Foods, Inc., a multimillion-dollar company that produces Honey Crème Syrup, Butter Pecan Syrup, and Maple Crème Syrup. She recently introduced a new low-carb product line, featuring Michele's Low Carb Honey Crème Surup and Butter Pecan Syrup as well as the Low Carb Pancake Mix and Michele's Classic Gourmet Pancake Mix. The company's products can be found in more than 10,000 food stores nationwide, including Stop & Shop, Super Wal*Mart, Albertson's, Kroger, Publix, Super Target, Cub Foods, H.E. Butt Grocery, Jewel Foods, Safeway, and Dominick's Finer Foods.

She was awarded the 2002 "Entrepreneur of the Year" award by the Women's Foodservices Forum, and she was the keynote speaker at Johnson & Wales University's commencement, at which time she received an honorary doctorate degree. She has been featured three times on *The Oprah Winfrey Show* and in other major media outlets, including CNN, Fox News, *People Magazine, Fortune,* and Black Entertainment Television (BET). *Dollars and Sense Magazine* voted her as one of the Top 100 Professional Women. Her other credits include *Black Enterprise Magazine*'s "The Emerging Company of the Year Award 1996," the Entrepreneurial Women Award in 1998, and the Madam Walker Entrepreneurial Award in 1999.

Michele has three daughters—Rosalyn, Christale, and Keisha—and one granddaughter, Lindsey. She lives in South Holland, IL.